In America

TALES FROM TRUMP COUNTRY

Caitríona Perry

Gill Books

Gill Books
Hume Avenue
Park West
Dublin 12
www.gillbooks.ie

Gill Books is an imprint of M.H. Gill and Co.

978 07171 7953 4

Print origination by O'K Graphic Design, Dublin
Edited by Emma Dunne

Maps adapted from iStock illustrations

Printed by CPI Group (UK), Croydon, CRO 4YY
This book is typeset in 12.5/17 pt Minion with chapter titles in Abolition.

The paper used in this book comes from the wood pulp of managed forests. For every tree felled, at least one tree is planted, thereby renewing natural resources.

A CIP catalogue record for this book is available from the British Library.

5 4 3 2 1

ACKNOWLEDGEMENTS

Everyone who told me their story, who let me into their home or workplace, who gave their honest and brave and sometimes unpopular opinions, and who shared the secrets of the ballot box. These are your stories and I hope I have done you some justice. And to all of those around the world who talk to journalists – thank you. Without you, there would be no us.

Deirdre Nolan, Sheila Armstrong, Teresa Daly and all at Gill Books. My literary agent Marianne Gunne O'Connor. All of my colleagues at RTÉ News, particularly those on the Foreign Desk, and Jon Williams. My journalistic colleagues here in the US with whom I shared this exhilarating journey. My wonderful friends, on both sides of the Atlantic. To my ever-supportive parents, beloved sisters and in-laws (and the technology that keeps us all connected). And above all, to my husband Rónán.

Rx.

CONTENTS

PREFACE

PREFACE

T ucking into a breakfast of shrimp and grits and stewed peaches on cinnamon-sugar-crunchy French toast, this former police chief and his wife are celebrating their fortieth wedding anniversary. Their three daughters chipped in to send them off for a night in this beautiful pre-American Revolution fort that is now a romantic, cosy inn in the middle of Mobile, Alabama.

Communal breakfast tables in romantic, cosy inns often make my heart sink. Sometimes the last thing you want to do first thing in the morning is talk to strangers. But more often than not, though, random chatter can turn up the most interesting nuggets of information.

It's not long after the 2016 presidential election so the conversation inevitably turns to the incoming forty-fifth president, Donald John Trump. They're diehard Republicans so naturally they voted for him. He wasn't their first choice, though. During the primary season they had favoured Ben Carson, the retired neurosurgeon with a colourful past, a man who was the butt of many of Trump's jokes at one time but later became a faithful supporter and is now Housing and Urban Development Secretary.

Discussing some of Trump's more controversial statements, they say not all of his tastes are their tastes. They're God-fearing people and have raised three professional daughters. They were always going to vote for the Republican candidate on the ticket, but they particularly like his position on the economy, and that he's pro-life, pro-guns and, most importantly, pro-Israel. I'm curious why they would rank his position on Israel so highly. Is the Palestinian–Israeli conflict such a hot topic so far down in the Deep South? No, their position is motivated by their love of the Bible, they say. They tell me they are Christians, and they believe that the Bible says all Christians should protect Israel no matter what. Trump says he will firmly support Israel and even wants to move the US embassy to Jerusalem – something no other country has done – so they are supporting him even though, as Christians, they don't like everything he stands for.

It's the first time I've heard such an argument from an American voter explaining their reasons for voting for Trump. But it shows how diverse America is. It is more akin to the European Union than it is to one particular country. You don't have to travel far in this vast nation to find yourself in a different land, where the food is different, the architecture is different, the climate is different, the industry is different, the language is different, the racial make-up is different, the attitude is different. And that is where the political problems come from. A strong argument can be made that the two-party system does not serve America well. It did not serve them well in picking the two candidates in 2016 – they had the lowest favourability ratings of any candidates ever going into polling day. It does not serve them well in attempting to put together a House and a Senate that serve all of the interests of all of the people and can actually pass legislation. And it left the door open for Trump, a man who was essentially an independent candidate running under the banner of the Republican Party – just as Bernie Sanders was an independent candidate running under the banner of the Democratic Party.

Without Barack Obama there would not have been a Donald Trump – the celebrity president, the unique president, the change candidate. Obama's successful argument in 2008 that people needed a break from the norm, that they should take a chance on him and come together, with people power, to change the nation, is a notion that Donald Trump piggy-backed on. Trump was viewed as the change candidate this time around; Hillary Clinton was the establishment candidate.

One of my predecessors in the role of RTÉ's Washington correspondent, Carole Coleman, may not have realised how prescient she was when she wrote in her 2008 book about what had brought about Barack Obama's election: 'Americans are ready for a new era of leadership. They are tired of mounting bills and stagnant wages, alarmed by illegal immigrants overwhelming their schools and hospitals, weary of war and being unloved abroad, and troubled by the increasing cost of health care and plummeting value of their homes.'[1]

All of these statements were still true of many Americans who went to the polls in November 2016. Except no matter how weary they had been in 2007 and 2008, they were even more so in 2016. More tired, more fed up. They'd given a chance to a traditional politician, to a Democrat, and that hadn't worked for them, so why not give a chance to an outsider? This manifested itself from the outset for both parties. Democrats, and some independent voters, suddenly found themselves drawn to Bernie Sanders – a long-time socialist who registered as a Democrat for the purposes of contesting the election. Republicans and other independent voters found themselves drawn to the other outsider candidate, Donald Trump.

Political commentators, and the Republican and Democratic party faithful alike, felt their heads spin on the night of 8 November 2016 as it became apparent that Donald Trump, the self-proclaimed billionaire businessman from a privileged background in New York, was on his way to becoming the forty-fifth president of the United States.

That shockwave rippled through much media coverage, in the US and abroad, and indeed in my own organisation, RTÉ, Ireland's public-service broadcaster. Researching this book, revisiting voters, rereading articles and polls, it's struck me that the world had been needlessly blindsided by the showmanship of Donald Trump. In many places the changing tide was there to see if people had looked closely enough. I felt the pull of the water when travelling around some of the states that Trump ultimately won and had been saying privately for about nine months that I thought it was possible he would do it, only feeling brave enough to say so on air about a week before his election. A reporter's gut instinct is something, but it's not enough to combat the seemingly strong argument of electoral-college maths equations and polls that were trending almost completely in one direction. There was no evidence other than the anecdotal evidence I was witnessing first hand. 'Report on the facts, not a feeling' is my creed.

I brought those voices and those stories to the people of Ireland (and further afield, thanks to the Internet) during 2015 and 2016. I felt an obligation to inform our audience of the opinions of voters that didn't coalesce with the pro-Democrat, pro-Clinton viewpoint that colours much of Western European political discourse. I was trying to remind people that in a two-horse race there is always a reasonable chance the so-called dark horse will win. Perhaps I succeeded a little; perhaps I failed miserably. If you're an eagle-eyed viewer of the RTÉ news, you'll have seen or heard from some of the characters on the following pages. Others are people I met in the course of my professional and personal travels. Some are people I've met since the election, as I returned to the key states in 2017 in my efforts to further understand what is happening right now in America. I asked everyone I met, respectfully, whom they had voted for. Most people told me honestly because I'm a foreigner, and although I'm a journalist, I don't work for a large US television network.

———

It is because I don't work for a large US television network that, in late June 2017, I found myself in the most unusual situation of my career to date – the subject of international attention and discourse following an encounter in the Oval Office with President Trump. In case you were tuned out of the constant Trump News Stream in the last week of June 2017, here's a quick recap of what happened: President Donald Trump was to have his first official phone call with the newly elected Taoiseach (Prime Minister) of Ireland, Leo Varadkar.

These phone calls are largely procedural; just a short call for introductions. I and the other members of the White House press corps had initially been told that there would be no media allowed at the event. In my role as Washington Correspondent for the national public broadcaster of Ireland, I had asked the White House Press Secretary Sean Spicer if he might supply me with a photograph of the call afterwards, as I knew this would be useful to our coverage given the nature of the call.

A short time before the call was due to take place, the White House got in touch with me and said that if I could get there quickly, I could film the call directly. I jumped in a cab and made the mile or so journey from my office to 1600 Pennsylvania Avenue in good time. Then the press pool was scrambled and we all gathered outside the Oval Office waiting on the call to start. The plan was that we would split into two groups of about ten, and we could film through the window of the Oval Office for a minute or so as President Trump spoke to Taoiseach Varadkar, which is the usual situation when the president is speaking to another world leader. However, as the first group approached the window, the door opened and we were beckoned inside. There were cameramen, still photographers, sound engineers and three or four reporters/correspondents, so up to maybe twenty members of the media in total, plus a few White House communications handlers, charged with getting us in and back out of the room.

When we entered the Oval Office, President Trump was on the phone with his desk diary open in front of him, playing with a white card that I believe had some talking points on it for the call to Ireland. Sitting across from him, and directly in front of me, were the National Security Adviser H.R. McMaster, the President's Chief Economic Adviser Gary Cohn, and Deputy National Security Adviser Dina Powell. There were a number of other presidential aides and advisers scattered throughout the room as well.

After about a minute and a half, a voice came across a speakerphone to say that the prime minister of Ireland, Taoiseach Leo Varadkar, was on the line. The two men then exchanged pleasantries, with President Trump congratulating Mr Varadkar on his 'great victory' – which was deemed a little unusual in Ireland, as Leo Varadkar became Taoiseach by a vote of the Fine Gael parliamentary party, and not by an election of the people. He won more weighty electoral college votes – but not more individual votes – than his rival Simon Coveney.

At this point the advisers started looking gingerly at the media, as if to say, 'Why are they still in here? We need to get to the substance of the call,' so the media handlers started ushering us out of the room. While this is done politely, it can at times feel a little aggressive. The president kept making small talk with the taoiseach, mentioning that there were lots of Irish press in the room – but there was just me. So, as the only Irish journalist in the room, I turned around upon his mention of 'Irish press'; a reflex action. We made eye contact, and the president clearly realised that as I had turned around I must be the Irish press. It was at this point he beckoned me over, wondering who I was. I have been criticised for going towards him when he curled his finger at me. To that I say – I was in the Oval Office, and he wanted to know who I was: a legitimate request.

The exchange went like this:

President Trump: 'We've got so many people from Ireland in this country. I know so many of them. I feel like I know all of them. I just want to congratulate you. That was a great victory that you had.'

Taoiseach Varadkar responds with something that we couldn't hear.

President Trump: 'We have a lot of your Irish press watching us … they're just now leaving the room.' Here, he spots me. 'And where are you from? Go ahead … come here, come here. We have all of this beautiful Irish press.'

Me: 'I'm from RTÉ News, the Taoiseach will know me. It's Caitríona Perry here, Taoiseach.'

President Trump: 'Caitriona Perry. She has a nice smile on her face so I bet she treats you well.'

I backed away from the desk quickly then, to audible chuckles from those in the room, because as much as I do want a one-on-one professional conversation with President Trump, to ask him the multitude of questions I have about his policies and his presidency, this was not the time. I was conscious that he had interrupted a conversation with another world leader to talk to me, and I certainly did not want to continue in a three-person dialogue, nor, I suspect, did anyone else want me to.

I had filmed the exchange on my mobile phone, as is customary practice for journalists nowadays, so we can tweet out images and video from a scene as quickly as possible, while better quality images and video are processed for broadcast shortly afterwards. Almost immediately, colleagues in the White House press corps began tweeting images. My own network, RTÉ, tweeted the mobile phone video I had filmed of the encounter and I later tweeted some of the pool footage too, describing it as a 'bizarre moment'. It was at that point that I began to 'go viral'.

As someone who has worked in the media for nearly two decades, it was most instructive to be the focus of such intense scrutiny. Articles and comments were published and broadcast about me right around the world. I had several hundred requests for interviews from what felt like every large media organisation I'd ever heard of, and many smaller ones I had never heard of.

There was much parsing of just what I had meant by the use of the word 'bizarre' to describe the moment. The Oxford dictionary definition of bizarre is 'very strange or unusual'. To my mind, the President of the United States interrupting a phone call with another world leader, in this case the Taoiseach of Ireland, the country where I'm from, to call over and speak to a journalist is bizarre – it is very strange and it is unusual. For me, the comments that the president made were secondary to this initial surprise at being beckoned as the media pool was being directed to leave the Oval Office. It is not the protocol I am used to. However, I am not used to being thrust into the international spotlight either!

There is a battle at play in the US at the moment involving the media. New media outlets and traditional media outlets are at war over ratings, access and verifiability. Right-wing outlets and left-wing outlets portray conflicting versions of the same events. And of course, since very early in the campaign, the president has been battling with the mainstream media (MSM). One can be cynical about that of course – it is somewhat of a win-win for all parties involved. The president scores bonus points with his base, while traditional media outlets are seeing record ratings and subscriptions at a time when audiences had begun to dwindle.

While the reaction to my interaction with President Trump was mostly positive, it was remarkable to note how easily media commentators in the US, Ireland, the UK and elsewhere jumped to assign motives both to me and to the president for our actions in that brief interaction. I was, by some accounts, 'asking' to be singled out by President Trump because I was wearing a red dress, and I'd only been appointed to such a prestigious role in the first place because I was 'a pretty young blonde'. By other accounts, I had been dreadfully 'demeaned' because the president had singled me out in front of a room full of senior administration, officials, fellow journalists and rolling TV cameras. Others said I had been subjected to extreme, albeit benign, sexism because my physical appearance, and not my professional achievements, had been commented on in a workplace by arguably the most powerful man in the world. Commentators talked about how upset and uncomfortable I had been, all without actually speaking to me. Others argued that there was something wrong with me because clearly, they said, I couldn't take a compliment. People said I was in the wrong because I didn't say thank you; others said I was in the wrong because I didn't reply with an expletive. An overwhelming number of women around the world contacted me to say they could identify with this sort of experience – unsolicited male attention.

I refused all interview requests at the time, because as evidenced from this sample of the polarised discourse, I was in a lose-lose situation. Yet the lack of input from me did not prevent the story being discussed ad nauseam, and the lack of original source material did not stop so many from assuming my viewpoint.

This is what I found fascinating. It was the one and only time in my life where I have been in sole posession of all of the facts of a story and could see how it played out across the media from that vantage point. It showed how polarised the media is here, and how agenda driven some outlets are. The president calling on a female reporter was shaped by some to perfectly feed a narrative about sexism and how badly he treats women. It was shaped by others to show that he doesn't hate all media, and can be very accommodating and charming to members of the press.

It is not for me to say what motivated his behaviour and whether he was setting out to be sexist. What I will say is that I did not feel 'demeaned'. After this long in the media business, I have developed a thick skin. As a female in a male-dominated environment, that was required a long time ago. A compliment from a much older gentleman, no matter the situation or power imbalance, does not have a negative impact on me. Brave and courageous female journalists around the world are sadly demeaned and violated in the truest sense of the words in their efforts to do their job, and I don't believe this incident in any way compares.

I think the president was trying to make small talk with the taoiseach, someone he had never met, while waiting for the media to leave the room so they could get into substantive matters. I think perhaps blondes catch his eye, and speaking with and complimenting an Irish reporter seemed like a good way at the time to strike some common ground with the taoiseach. I think as the only Irish journalist in the room, I was possibly the only person he didn't recognise. I think he has such a well-documented history, and such negative associations with women, that it fed a certain narrative. I think had Bill Clinton said the same thing to a female reporter in the Oval Office, the same negative narrative would have been fuelled. If Barack Obama or George W. Bush (or any world leader) had interrupted their conversation with the taoiseach to call me over, I would have viewed it in an equally bizarre and odd light. I do think, however, it is probably not something that would have happened with any other recent US president, because they were traditional politicians aware of traditional protocols. But if there is one thing we've learned from President Trump in these past two years, it is that he tore up the rulebook some time ago.

———

This book was written and completed months before that Oval Office incident. It is not a state-by-state guide or a breakdown as to how people voted in the election. It's about the particular states and the types of people who helped get Donald Trump elected. The true red states that always vote Republican did so this time around, and the true-blue states that always vote Democrat did so too. Here I'm looking at the purple states, or the sky-blue and baby-pink states, that can often lean a certain way but ultimately fall in the other direction – as they did in November 2016. I focus heavily on the Appalachian states, the so-called Rust Belt region. This is also what Trump did. He tapped into that zeitgeist of unfulfilled potential, of overbearing frustration, and gave the people what they wanted. As a veteran businessman, he saw a gap in the market and went for it – 'big league'.

There's an honourable mention too, in this book, for the Irish Americans who supported Trump, although nobody can claim they won the election for him. There's no exit poll data to show just how the Irish American vote was cast, but as Donald Trump won the majority of white Catholic voters, one has to assume that many of those were Irish Americans. Although in Ireland we have the impression that there remains an 'Irish voting bloc' in US politics, it has been my experience that American politicians do not view it that way – neither the Republicans nor the Democrats approach Irish Americans nationally as a group. On a local level, there are Irish Democratic strongholds and Irish Republican strongholds but neither is capable of swinging a presidential election one way or another. Rather than being 'Irish American voters', they are just 'voters', with the same concerns and variances as any others. And while there are a great many Irish Americans in politics and public service in general, they are pretty evenly spread on both sides of the aisle.

But a final note. This book is not intended to tell you why people didn't vote for Donald Trump. Those reasons are obvious and indeed well-documented: 58 per cent of women didn't, 92 per cent of black people didn't, 71 per cent of Hispanic people didn't, 42 per cent of white people didn't, 55 per cent of those who were college educated didn't.[2] Their reasons ranged from being staunch Democrats to being offended by his comments on immigrants, Latinos, those with disabilities, women and more. We know a lot about why people didn't vote for him. This book is about why people did. This book is about explaining the good that people see in Donald Trump. It's about looking at why individuals can overlook racist and sexist comments and behaviour, overlook the lack of tax returns and so on, to see a man they wanted as president. A man they still want as president. You know why people didn't vote for Donald Trump: now meet some of the ones who did.

Caitríona Perry

July 2017

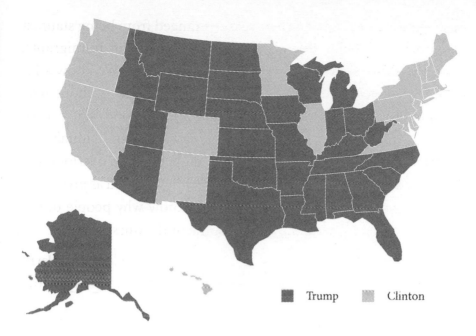

States won by each candidate in the 2016 US presidential election

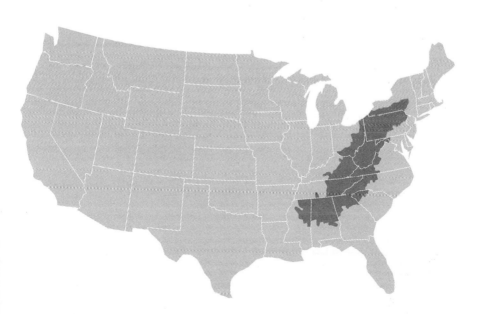

The Appalachian region

Introduction

AS GOES OHIO, SO GOES THE NATION

Danelle is enrolled in the same course as her mom. They're both studying to be pharmacy technicians. Danelle is twenty-one and her mom – well, let's just say she's not twenty-one. They live in Portsmouth, Ohio. It's called Portsmouth not because it's a coastal port but because in the days of barges and shipping it was a major port on the River Ohio, looking across at Kentucky, right in the middle of the Appalachian region. The mighty river is the state line.

Danelle is a beautiful, composed and articulate young woman. Her story, though, is an all too familiar one here.

She's that girl you see in every American high-school movie: the stereotypical beauty, smart and pretty, with the lovely boyfriend, who is friends with everyone. Straight after she left high school, though, Danelle got pregnant and so she put off her education 'for a little bit'. She worked in Walmart and was a customer-service manager there. But 'I just wanted to get back to school'. Her daughter is two now, 'So it's the perfect time to go back,' she says.

Portsmouth is typical of many places in the so-called Rust Belt region. Once a big trading town, a big factory town, it was busy and populated. But then industrialisation happened, and then globalisation happened, and then technological advancements happened, and suddenly the traditional jobs that had employed generations of families were gone.

The tale is not unique to Ohio, not unique to neighbouring Pennsylvania, not strictly unique to the Midwest, the Heartland, and definitely not unique to the United States. But it is in many ways the story of the Appalachian region.

Ohio is one of the thirteen American states that make up that region, home to some twenty-five million people, most of whom are statistically living close to or below the poverty line. Broadly speaking, it follows the spine of the Appalachian Mountains from southern New York along a rough diagonal to northern Mississippi, taking in Alabama, Georgia, Kentucky, Maryland, North Carolina, Ohio, Pennsylvania, South Carolina, Tennessee, Virginia and West Virginia (the only state which falls entirely in Appalachia).

Danelle has a big test this morning but she's as cool as the proverbial cucumber – nervous about chatting to a journalist, for sure, but the exam will be a doddle. I'm worried that because she's anxious about talking to me, things may not go as well in the exam as she'd planned. But she reassures me she has it 'in the bag'.

She says she chose to study pharmacy tech because she 'just wanted to go and help people'. So far, her bedside manner seems top notch. She also wanted to get into the medical sphere because it is 'probably one of the best jobs to go in to. Medical is really the best field around here. And electricity. I'm studying pharmacy technician because it has a lot of job opportunity in this area.'

Many of her peers working in other industries have had to move away for work. But most of her friends are in medical and electricity. 'Or cops! I don't know why, but that seems to be a big thing.' She adds, 'I know a lot of people who go into the military.' Some 3.7 per cent of people in Ohio aged between eighteen and twenty-four join the military, which may not seem like a lot, but is the eighth highest youth enlistment rate of all of the fifty states.

Twenty-one-year-old Kody Millar is also looking for a job in the medical field. A tall, strapping young man who looks as if he just walked in from American football training, he is studying a course in practical nursing. He wants, ultimately, to become a certified registered nurse anaesthetist, so he has to become an advanced practice nurse in anaesthesiology. It's going to take six more years of school. 'I've got a lot of years still ahead of me,' he jokes, but 'this is a fantastic place to start.' He's talking about the Scioto County Career Technical Center training school. It's very similar to an Irish College of Further Education but is a fairly unique concept in American education. In fact, its superintendent (head of school), Stan Jennings, has come to Ireland on visiting missions before. Its focus, though, is extremely industry-centric. It offers short courses to train the area's young people specifically for the needs of the area's jobs. A clever concept, if a little reactionary. But in a country with 70.8 million young people and a virtually non-existent welfare system, work is everything.

Take our nurse anaesthetist hopeful, Kody. He spent six or seven months studying welding first. Not exactly a similar skill set. He really liked it but he changed for one reason: 'you have to go here and there to get a job. There's just nothing really local. You get laid off a lot.' So why nursing? 'This is more of a steady job and I think it will be … eh, I like it very well so far.'

Travelling for work is the way of life for the young, and not so young, lucky enough to have a job in this area. According to the Appalachian Regional Commission, the body charged with improving and developing the region, 41 per cent of the population live in rural areas, compared with 20 per cent of the whole US population.

Portsmouth, though, is something of a hub town for southern Ohio, which is evidenced in its medical facilities, as Kody explains.

'You have SOMC [Southern Ohio Medical Center] just right down the road. That's a major hospital for southern Ohio. You have King's Daughters Medical Center [over the border in Kentucky]. You have a lot of urgent cares and medical centres and stuff. I think you can always find a job in medical.'

He does say that industry in general has 'kind of dropped off' around southwestern Ohio, as in a lot of the United States, but excitedly says that they're building a bypass on the edge of the town and there are lot of jobs in that.

Set against a rural background, with a mineral-rich mountain range and mostly fertile farmland, it is not surprising that traditionally the economy in the region was driven almost exclusively by mining, forestry and agriculture, and by chemical and heavy industries. It has become more diversified in recent times, with manufacturing and professional services moving in, but the move away from those traditional land-based industries has caused much of the economic depression in the region in the past generation or two.

The impact has been dramatic. The average unemployment rate in Appalachia is higher than the national figure. The number of people living below the poverty line is higher than the US average. Fewer people have completed high school education, and fewer have received a bachelor's degree than the national average. A much higher percentage of the population in Appalachia is white. There are also more older people and fewer young people in the region compared to the US average, showing the impact the sustained economic depression is having on migration trends and the region's future prospects. A lack of opportunities means youth making the transition to adulthood are moving out of the region, perhaps never to return.

Kody and Danelle are standing in one of the practical medical-training rooms, complete with a disturbingly lifelike 'dummy'. The next building over houses all of the trades and crafts.

The welding room is hot and noisy. About thirty cubicles line the perimeter of the room. Each contains a student in fully protective clothing, armed with a blow-torch. Sparks are flying in every direction. Here, Kody and Danelle's fellow student Nathan Sexton is training to be a welder and, unlike them, his plan is to get as far away as he can as soon as possible. He wants to head to the 'pipeline out west' – the Keystone pipeline.

Stalled by Obama, reactivated by Trump once in office, the pipeline would link oil producers in Canada and North Dakota with oil refinery plants and export terminals on the Gulf Coast, allowing for fast, more efficient and competitive exports. On President Trump's instruction, the State Department granted TransCanada a construction licence in February 2017. His predecessor, then President Barack Obama, had rejected the project in late 2015. He accepted the weighty environmental arguments for refusing it and felt it would undermine the global leadership that the United States was trying to show in moving away from a reliance on fossil fuels. But that was then, and this is now. It's a new America.

Eighteen-year-old Nathan had been studying at his local high school, where he was doing mostly welding, but transferred to the Scioto County Career Technical Center to focus on his welding skills. Here he does three hours a day of just welding, and the rest of the time he studies the regular curriculum. He feels the ability to focus is really important because he's learning a trade, as he puts it, 'that's going to feed me for most of my life … that's pretty much it'. He wants to be a pipefitter.

He says there aren't as many jobs for pipefitters in southwestern Ohio as there might be in other parts of the country, so he's getting ready to up sticks and leave as soon as he gets his technical qualification. He does point out that you can make a living in Ohio, but not the kind he wants. 'It's perfectly fine here, but I'm going after more of a … eh … well, I'm young and I really have nothing keeping me here so I can go and work in other places, make more money and then I can come back here and settle.'

He's an ambitious guy, with big plans for his future. There's a lot of talk about Trump in his community, but when I met him a week or so out from the election, he didn't plan on voting at all. 'I really don't think we have many options this election. I'm just not much into it I guess.' He's going to determine his own fate through hard work and not rely on any politician to fix things for him.

Superintendent Stan Jennings is the driving force at this training centre. He's a visionary, a principal, a negotiator, a fundraiser and a friendly face all rolled into one. He appears to know every student here by name. He's one of those vocational teachers, devoting his life to bettering the future of the young people of his area. He sees what's on the horizon in Southwest Ohio. He sees the unemployment. He sees the drugs. He sees the teenage pregnancies, the single-parent families, the low-income families, the multi-generational poverty, and he wants to make a change for those coming into adulthood now.

Stan Jennings explains that about 70 per cent of the jobs in the area are ones that require what he calls 'skill sets'. 'They don't necessarily need a bachelor's degree or a master's degree: they need skill sets.' Young people that come straight from a traditional high school 'are still lacking skill sets', he says, 'so their employment potential is extremely low'.

His students are work-ready. So much so that he says he generally has jobs ready for about 80 per cent of those who graduate at high-school level and 90 per cent of those who do the two years of further training.

This helps boost the area in two ways, he says. When a student leaves here with work lined up, it obviously has enormous benefits for the young person's sense of self-worth and also keeps the area going through that person's ability to support themselves. They're contributing to society and being kept away from the cliff's edge of drug addiction that is so pervasive in this state and many others.

But Jennings also says that businesses and industries are attracted to the area 'for the simple reason we've got the workforce they need to make their businesses successful'.

And he's understandably proud of what he's achieved. 'I don't know how you can do much better in an area where people say there's no jobs but I'm leaving jobs on the table because I don't have enough students in my pipeline.'

He's coy about his own personal political preferences and says it doesn't matter to the community's projects who is the leader of the country. 'We can be fairly self-sufficient here,' he says, 'we can create our own vehicles here, we can build our own houses here.' And indeed they can. The back car-park of the school building has a timber-frame house that the students are building from scratch. They have all the requisite tradespeople there for the construction, and they have furniture makers and interior-design students for the inside. They'll eventually sell it as part of the fundraising efforts for the facility. The same is true of some of the vintage cars on the lot. They salvage scrap from junk yards and rebuild and recondition the vehicles until they're shiny and new, and sell them on again to help the school. It's quite an enterprise. And there's a culinary course where, among other things, those students make, bottle and sell locally a rather exquisite barbecue sauce.

Jason Kester is executive director of the Southern Ohio Port Authority. He's charged with redeveloping the region, cleaning up derelict neighbourhoods and attracting back industry, and maybe even boosting tourism. It's a fantastically beautiful part of the country, and for a European tourist, something completely undiscovered.

Portsmouth itself has a picturesque park, bounded by the Ohio River, where you can look across at Kentucky. The number-one tourist destination in the area, according to reviewers on TripAdvisor, is a flood wall mural. It is pretty impressive, and the artwork tells its own story, but it is still a wall.

Jason and his team are working hard for the region in the same spirit as Stan Jennings – to make Portsmouth and South Ohio as attractive as possible. When Donald Trump follows through on his promise of 'bringing back the jobs', they want to make sure they're ready to receive them.

But Jason is clear on what the biggest issue right across the region is at the moment: 'A lack of sites and buildings.'

'By that I mean a site with suitable capacities of water, sewer, natural gas, fibre and electric for commercial/industrial development. In Cincinnati or Topeka or wherever you have industrial or business parks with buildings constructed by private developers to house business and industry. Across Southeast Ohio we have brownfields and cornfields. The locales with industrial parks are doing great, those that don't generally … aren't. It's what we're struggling with right now – developing a new industrial park since our parks are now full.'

Back at the welding workshop, though, Nathan wants more than Appalachia can offer him. At $56,520 the average family income is nearly $10,000 less here than the national average. In a recent report, the Appalachian Regional Commission concluded that family and household income rates in the region have not yet returned to where they were in 2005, before the recession struck. That's over twenty-five million people in thirteen states who are still worse off now than they were twelve years ago. These people have already experienced generations of changing technologies taking jobs done by humans and giving them to robots, and still the money they have to live on is less now than more than a decade ago. These people are fed up and angry and need someone to blame. Of course they are. Of course they do.

Enter Donald Trump. He saw the anger and the destitution in this group of older, whiter, poorer, less-well-educated people in this part of the country and targeted them with his presidential campaign. His messages spoke directly to them, more so than any other broad group of people anywhere else in the US. Ten of the thirteen states that make up Appalachia voted for Trump. Without them he certainly would not have won the election. Pennsylvania was among those Appalachian States that delivered a Trump victory, but it – like Wisconsin and Michigan – flipped from being a Democratic-voting state to a Republican one with such a narrow margin of victory that things could easily have ended quite differently.

But while Stan Jennings might be keeping his political cards close to his chest, his training centre is deep in Trump country. Donald Trump ran away with the vote here. He won Scioto County with a 33 per cent margin of victory. By comparison, the 2012 Republican candidate, Mitt Romney, beat Barack Obama here by a mere 1.9 per cent. Interestingly, unlike other parts of the state where the total turnout was different, here Hillary Clinton got 5,300 fewer votes than Barack Obama, and Donald Trump got 5,527 more votes than Romney. Nobody's suggesting that the same 5,000 voters who saw something good in Obama then saw that same thing in Trump. But some of them must have. For as Barack Obama promised a brighter future and offered hope, so too did Donald Trump. That brighter future didn't come here under Obama so, to a voter's mind, what evidence did they have that it would come with Hillary Clinton at the helm instead?

But what is really interesting is what happened with young people like those working here in the welding room, the trainee radiology technicians, the carpenters, the plumbers – the so-called millennials.

Overall, Donald Trump fared quite poorly with young people. Only about a third of those aged under thirty voted for him. But of the young people who did vote for him, three-quarters did so because they felt he could bring 'needed change', somewhat reminiscent of Barack Obama's message that saw young people come out in their droves in 2008. Exit polls showed a surge of young, white, male conservative voters. A signal for future elections, perhaps?

There is a saying in American politics: 'As goes Ohio, so goes the nation.' It's hackneyed because it's true. No Republican candidate has ever been elected president without winning Ohio, and no

Democrat since John F. Kennedy has won without the Buckeye State either.

Ohio played a significant role in the 2016 campaign. The state held its primary on 15 March and its governor John Kasich won 46.6 per cent of the vote, with Donald Trump winning 35.9 per cent. When Kasich bowed out of the race, leaving Trump the last man standing, and continued with a vehement anti-Trump message, it was unclear what would happen in Ohio at general election time. Would the people stick with their governor and follow his lead or vote for Trump anyway?

Later, in July, Ohio played host to the Republican National Convention, and at the end of a week of pomp and pageantry boycotted by many senior Republicans, including the party's last two presidents, the red, white and blue balloons dropped, the streamers swung, the music played and Donald Trump was named the Republican Party's official nominee to contest the election.

But the voters in Ohio were key to the campaign too – both in their own right as an important swing state to win and as a bellwether for many other states with similar populations.

Ohio brings the story of Donald Trump and the Republicans full circle. Without winning the primary, without the support or even the personal vote of the state's Republican governor, on election night, 8 November 2016, Trump won the state of Ohio, as he would say himself, 'big league' (or is it 'bigly'?) with the biggest victory margin there in twenty-eight years. He won eighty of the eighty-eight counties in the Buckeye state. In thirty of them, he got at least 70 per cent of the vote – a resounding victory in the popular vote there, if not across the country as a whole.

The eighteen electoral votes he won in Ohio helped bring him over the magical number of 270, the majority of the 538 electoral-college votes available to win the presidency.

The system designed by the Founding Fathers to select the nation's president is somewhat complicated. It was designed to ensure that smaller states with particular interests would not be ignored or swept up in the desires of bigger urban areas. Although the concept is admirable, in practice, in the modern era, it does not exactly preserve the parity that it was originally designed to guarantee. While it continues to prevent smaller rural areas being swallowed up by larger urban areas, it has swung too much in the other direction. The voters in smaller areas and in the so-called swing states have a disproportionate say in the result.

To explain, the US president is not elected technically by the people, but rather by the 538 electors who make up the electoral college. They meet after polling day to cast votes based on how the voters in their individual states have voted.

That figure of 538 is the product of a maths equation. Each of the fifty states starts off with two votes – one for each of its senators. Each state then gets a varying number of extra votes to equal the number of members it has in the House of Representatives – those seats themselves based on population. So that's another 435 electors. Then three electors are allocated for the District of Columbia – the special status area is the nation's capital but because it's not a state it does not have any senators and has only one non-voting delegate to the House of Representatives. So that makes 538 members of the electoral college – a majority of 270 is needed to win.

In all bar two states, all of the allocated votes go to the person who gets the biggest popular vote. This means that even if the race is really close and one candidate only wins a state by less than 1 per cent, they still win all of the electoral-college votes. Maine and Nebraska award their electors proportionately – the nearest thing to the Irish system of proportional representation.

The maths of how states would vote in 2016 appeared to be stacked against Donald Trump. There were simply more electoral-college votes in staunchly Democratic states or those that tended to lean Democratic. From the outset he was said to face an uphill battle to flip those states that, in recent years, had usually leaned Democratic. But therein lies the conceit – 'usually'. There was nothing usual about this election.

In thirty-eight states, voters can cast their votes ahead of the actual polling day. This means that scandals and fluffs that occur late in the campaign sometimes do not have the dramatic impact that they might have in another jurisdiction. In 2016, for example, by the time it got to polling day, more than half of the voters in Nevada and Florida had already cast their votes.

For this and many other reasons, relying on polling – an inexact science at the best of times – was precarious for this election. It became evident early on that nothing about the 2016 campaign was inevitable. It was the most surprising, thrilling, caustic, nasty, exhausting, exhilarating contest in recent memory. It left chests puffed up and heads cast down. It highlighted the deep divisions that exist in America. Now this country, as wonderful as it is, perhaps has more that divides its people than unites them. The election of President Barack Obama, the country's first African American president, was supposed to unify. It was supposed to bookend the dark history of slavery and generations of racism. Instead, in many ways, it showed how that era is not over and how, arguably, he left behind a more divided country than the one he inherited.

Those divisions were further highlighted in the wake of the election of Donald Trump. He won the race by winning a majority of the electoral-college votes – in accordance with the wishes of the Founding Fathers – but not a majority of the votes of the actual population. In not winning the popular vote, by losing that contest by a margin of nearly three million people, President Trump took office knowing that more people didn't vote for him than did. And the people of America saw a president take office knowing that more people didn't vote for him than did.

———

Cleveland, Ohio is a city of many sides. Driving in from the airport you see the literal rust belt: buildings falling down, once fabulous structures crumbling – a theme throughout this part of the country. There's graffiti, there's litter, there are feral cats and mangy dogs and probably many more vermin that are, thankfully, not immediately apparent. It really doesn't look like a place you'd want to stop. But there is a certain charm in the rustic industrial appearance. If the buildings were churches they'd look romantic, but because they're factories they look like eyesores.

Go on a little further and you come to Lake Erie and the Cuyahoga River. This was known as the Burning River for decades because it was so polluted that on 22 June 1969 sparks from a passing train set fire to oil-soaked debris in the river near a steel mill, a fire which quickly spread. It caused about $100,000 worth of damage to two railroad bridges. The fire was put out in about half an hour but the story lived on and, at the time, sparked environmental activism. It wasn't the first time the river had caught fire – it had also happened in 1952, engulfing a ship in flames. Factories and residential areas just dumped their waste straight into the river. Nothing was treated. There was no fish or plant life in the river. The story of the Burning River led to the creation of the Environmental Protection Agency and later the introduction of the Clean Water Act. It's been transformed in the nearly forty years since, with part of the river fully restored and home once again to fish and wildlife.

Then you arrive in shabby-chic Cleveland, a really vibrant arts district filled with fantastic restaurants and wonderfully repurposed structures – like the Crop Bistro, housed in a 1925 United Bank building. An austere, large space, it was closed down four years after it opened, such was the impact of the Great Depression. The Burning River incident has been turned around into a great boon for the city. The Great Lakes Brewing Company now makes Burning River Pale Ale, which it describes itself as 'a toast to the Cuyahoga River Fire'. With a flavour that's described as 'igniting the senses and not our local waterways', it has won several awards at the World Beer Championships, putting Cleveland on the craft brew map.

Property too tells a tale here. A large family home in the artists' district – four bedrooms, 2,500 square feet on a quarter of an acre with a sculpted garden with menagerie and hot tub – costs $127,000. That's about $50 per square foot – the median US price per square foot is $132.

Barack Obama won Ohio in 2008 and again in 2012 although only by 2.98 percentage points. But that Democratic support swung right around to the Republican Party – Hillary Clinton lost the state in 2016 by 8.1 percentage points. She held Cleveland, winning more than twice the number of votes that Donald Trump did, but it just wasn't enough to take the state. And even though she won Cleveland, the Democratic party need to beware for the future, as her turnout was much lower than that of Obama.

Don't be fooled. America is not all fast cars, shining buildings, ostentatious wealth, designer clothes and coiffed hairstyles. Its current first family may be all that, but the people who put them there are not. The United States is a wonderful place. It's a meritocracy. It's a place where you can pull yourself up by your bootstraps to a certain extent – though you will need luck, the kindness of others and the ability to work two or three jobs at once. And for many people, that is impossible. Poverty traps, vicious drug cycles and small-town backwaters are the extent of their futures. Protesting is for 'fancy folk' in Washington DC. An average working week is sixty hours, not forty hours, and the Affordable Care Act (with or without the Obama prefix) is potentially all that's keeping people from bankruptcy and/or homelessness should they or their family members get sick.

If you take a map showing the states with the highest numbers of people living below the poverty line and a map showing the states that voted for Donald Trump and line them up on top of each other, they are almost identical.[3] As Richard Florida puts it in his thesis on what he calls the New Urban Crisis: 'The very same clustering force that generates economic and social progress [in cities] also divides us ... as more and more middle class neighbourhoods fade, our cities, suburbs, and nation as a whole are splintered into a patchwork of concentrated advantage and concentrated disadvantage.'[4]

This clustering effect can be seen in wealthy areas of New York, Washington DC, San Francisco, Chicago, Los Angeles and many other places. The really rich surround each other and many have no real comprehension of 'how the other half live'. These wealthy elites often set the political agenda, most explicitly because they can donate large sums of money to candidates and parties. They can essentially buy influence through lobbying. They don't understand the lives of people living somewhere like Appalachia and, with some exceptions, perhaps care little.

Although Donald Trump grew up in a wealthy household, went to good schools, went to work with his father earning a good salary and has never had to worry about where his next meal is coming from or if he has a warm coat and boots for winter, he connects with people who have none of his privilege and all of those worries. He's straight talking. He doesn't use fancy words. He speaks in simple language. His election slogans were straightforward and memorable. He uses slang and common parlance. He talks 'dirty' on occasion – remember the *Access Hollywood* 'grabbing' tape? He talks 'mean' on occasion – as evidenced in the election-campaign debates: the tone was lowered there like never before in an election cycle. He wears a baseball cap with an ill-fitting suit and a wind-defying comb-over. There is nothing 'fancy' in his appearance. He, in many ways, is the everyman – and yet in no way is he the everyman.

But somehow, to Americans in small farmhouses, big ranches, trailer parks and apartment blocks across the nation, he spoke to the 'ordinary' people in a way that Hillary Clinton could only dream of. The Independent Senator turned Democratic Party member Bernie Sanders did it a little too but, ultimately, he did not have the fortune and business empire that Trump sat on. That wealth, that self-sufficiency, appealed in a material way to voters in a country where success and self-improvement are inspirational qualities. Talking about the American Dream was one thing, living it was another.

Donald Trump is the ultimate empire-builder, the man who took bricks and mortar and, through hard dealing and sometimes little regard for those who got in his way, built glittering, glistening towers of gold (or at least bronze-toned glass).

The question that dominated discussion during the election, the question that still occupies the minds of Democrats, the chattering classes and many people around the world, is how could people who have absolutely nothing in common with Donald Trump vote for him? How could they see in him something they could not see in the other Republican primary candidates and in Hillary Clinton? Something they did not see in Barack Obama? This question strikes repeatedly as you tour the communities who voted for Trump, meet these people and get to know them.

The answer is not straightforward, but there are three things to consider.

First, it stems from the hunt for the American Dream. That may seem like an over-simplification but, ultimately, people here strive to better themselves and better their offspring. That is most certainly not exclusively a financial betterment: it can also be ideological or holistic. Donald Trump offered that, something fresh and new. Hillary Clinton, on the other hand, offered more of the same. By not being populist enough, by being too Obama-ish, she actually lost, rather than gained, advantage.

The American Dream is the recurring theme among Trump voters – a sense of hope that the future will and should be better. It is the same strand of hope that Barack Obama offered, described here in his victory speech in Chicago after the 2012 election.

> America, I believe we can build on the progress we've made and continue to fight for new jobs and new opportunities and new security for the middle class. I believe we can keep the promise of our founding, the idea that if you're willing to work hard, it doesn't matter who you are or where you come from or what you look like or who you love. It doesn't matter whether you're black or white or Hispanic or Asian or Native American or young or old or rich or poor, abled, disabled, gay or straight. You can make it here in America if you're willing to try.

It is that hope, that chance that it could be you, that spurs many voters to evaluate candidates based on how likely they are to make improvements for them. When blue-collar, white workers in middle America look at Donald Trump in his ill-fitting suit and baseball cap, with a physical image that is perhaps more like their own, they see a possibility that they could be him. Aside from his skin colour, Barack Obama, with his lean physique, good looks and charisma, hanging out with rock stars and movie stars, his life and what he stands for seems at a far remove. Except the reality is that he was raised without his father, cared for by his grandparents and moved around a lot as a child, meaning he has potentially much more in common with the Appalachian voters than Donald Trump. He lived and achieved the American Dream in arguably a more fundamental way than Trump did.

But because people think the American Dream entitles them to the right to achieve something better in life, it can lead to anger and frustration when it doesn't happen. This is why the Democrats and Obama were blamed for the lack of sufficient recovery from the economic recession. (Although it is important to note that each time a party has been in office for two terms in a row, there is an established pattern where they lose power to the other party, as citizens have had enough.)

Robert Kraft, the owner of the New England Patriots, brought his team to celebrate their Super Bowl victory at the White House on 19 April 2017. That game was the first ever Super Bowl to go into overtime. The Patriots came from twenty-five points behind to win by six points – the biggest comeback in Super Bowl history. American sports history is populated with stories of sportsmen and women who have overcome adversity in their early lives to be some of the wealthiest people in the country. Their personal stories inspire the American Dream narrative as well, as did that epic Patriots comeback. Standing on the grounds of the White House, Robert Kraft, an early and vocal supporter of Donald Trump, put that spirit in words. 'Overcoming long odds through hard work, perseverance and mental toughness is the foundation of everything that is great about this country,' he said.

The second reason people voted for Trump is that because he doesn't really stand *for* anything in particular, he *can* stand for anything. He was somewhat of an à-la-carte candidate. Because he chopped and changed his positions and didn't lay anything out in great detail the way Clinton did, voters could pick and choose what they did and didn't like about him. And, hey, you're never going to totally *love* a candidate and everything about them, are you? It's always going to be quid pro quo. Because Donald Trump never outlined his true feelings on anything in more detail than a soundbite or a couple of paragraphs of a speech, voters could interpret for themselves what he meant. They could project on him what they wanted him to stand for and ignore the parts they didn't.

The ideology of Obama hadn't worked out, so now it was time for realism and commercialism. The rights of the individual came ahead of the interests of the collective. Trump may not be the kind of man you want to hang out with, and he may do untold damage to the US and its reputation, he may destroy the world order, but there was a belief that he would improve my lot in life, and your lot in life, and our neighbours' lots and so on.

The extremely religious evangelicals who live their lives in strict accordance with the teachings of the Bible, and forsake all else, voted in their droves for the thrice-married, self-confessed womanising playboy billionaire. According to the national exit poll, eight out of ten white self-identified born-again or evangelical Christians told pollsters they had voted for Donald Trump. On the face of it, that is a contradictory stance. However, for many voters, faced with two candidates they didn't particularly like, they voted on single issues. In the case of the evangelical voters, that was abortion.

As in every election in the US, a candidate's position on abortion will make up many a voter's mind. In this case, Donald Trump said he was pro-life. This meant that evangelical voters could pick this option from his á-la-carte menu of positions. In particular, during the third presidential debate, when Hillary Clinton said she would protect the landmark *Roe v Wade* decision which allows abortion in every state, Donald Trump said he would do everything he could to get it overturned. He used emotive language about late-term abortions, saying, 'It's not OK with me, because based on what she's saying, and based on where she's going, and where she's been, you can take the baby and rip the baby out of the womb in the ninth month on the final day. And that's not acceptable.'

The comments he made during that debate came so late in the election cycle that they could leave voters with no doubt as to his position, especially as he had said previously that he was pro-choice (1999), pro-life with exceptions (2016), and open to leaving the situation was it was (2016). But this categoric final position on abortion allowed religious voters of both parties to cast their vote for him with a clear conscience.

The third reason for the success of Trump's campaign is that there was an appetite for a backlash, a punishment vote. Those same people who felt left out of the economic recovery, who felt ignored by the traditional politicians of Washington DC, wanted to make that establishment, those career politicians of all colours, feel some of the pain and suffering that the American people had been feeling. They couldn't understand why economic improvements were not the priority. It made no sense to them that politicians were concerning themselves with debates over which bathroom a transgender schoolchild could use. Civil rights like those should come secondary to economic stability, they believed.

There is a reason why a disproportionate number of white people voted for Donald Trump. The Civil Rights Movement was not that long ago. Racism is enshrined in many parts of daily life in the US. Some of those white people living in predominantly white areas fear they are being outnumbered. In 2016, for the first time more Hispanic babies were born in the US than white babies. The generation currently being born is 48 per cent white; my generation in the US is 61 per cent white and my parents' generation is 81 per cent white. That diminishing position of dominance, the changing demographics due to the influx of Asian and Hispanic immigrants, has confused some people. They are feeling threatened both financially and culturally. Suddenly, the immigrants they lived alongside their whole lives became the Other. If their lot is not improving, it must be the fault of those arriving into the country, reducing opportunities for those born here (although this ignores the point that many immigrants do the jobs that American-born workers won't do, such as farm labouring, dishwashing, housekeeping etc.). If there is suddenly no way to improve one's economic standing, it must be someone's fault, and so it became the fault of people who looked different. This is where Trump's anti-immigrant message struck such a chord. He made it OK to say out loud what had been kept to a whisper between only the closest of like-minded individuals.

After the election of November 2016, the United States was more divided than ever. In many families, Thanksgiving two weeks later became a family day to avoid rather than excitedly anticipate, as dinner-table conversations would inevitably turn nasty if some of the family had voted for Trump and others had voted for Clinton. Some friends had to agree to not discuss politics in social settings as the trauma felt by Democrats in those first days was too difficult to manage. In the twenty-four hours immediately after the election, I saw a least a dozen people openly crying on the streets of Washington DC, equating their post-election feeling to grief.

'Oh Me Oh My Oh, would you look at Miss Ohio' goes a famous Americana bluegrass song. It's about a beauty queen who is deemed a little too unsavoury for the pageant judges. She throws off what she sees as the shackles of convention with a burning desire to just do what she wants. She's beset by scandal but beloved. As the song goes, people don't like her but are drawn to her and keep staring nonetheless. She's captivating and, as the last verse reveals, she has some baggage she needs to deal with, but it's not entirely clear just what that baggage is.

Written years before Trump's run for the presidency, the song could be an allegorical tale. Reality-TV star Trump wins the Republican Party crown in Ohio at a national convention boycotted by most of the elite and establishment branch of the party, including the Ohio governor, such is their disgust and unease at Trump and the notion that he would be their flag-bearer. Donald J. Trump is the phenomenon that people could not take their eyes off, whether or not they wanted to.

Pennsylvania

THE REALLY RUSTY RUST BELT

The black and white tiles on the floor have seen plenty of footfall. But not today. There are more plastic flowers in the window of this Western Pennsylvania diner than there are customers in the lunchtime 'rush'.

It looks exactly like hipster hotspots in Brooklyn, San Francisco and parts of Washington DC: a place that has a shabby-chic retro feel and is frequented by millennials, a place that looks like a 1950s diner but serves crispy kale and cold-brewed coffee – and knows how to charge for it. This is not that place. This looks like a 1950s diner because it is a 1950s diner. Its kitsch style is its original style. The menus are wipe-clean laminated sheets of printed paper. You can order crispy French fries and cold-cuts of meat. And burgers – the staple of cafes and diners across the US. (There should be a footnote in the job description for any foreign correspondent coming to America – 'Must have an insatiable appetite for twenty-four-hour news … and burgers.') It's cheap here, a burger and fries for $7. It has to be: the minimum wage in Pennsylvania is set at the federal rate of $7.25 per hour.

The bathroom, or restroom, is downstairs in a basement area that is part staff break area, part storage room for giant tins of tomatoes and packets of salt and drums of canola oil. A wooden shutter at the bottom of the stairs shields the toilet bowl from the world and offers privacy for ablutions. It reminds me of the outdoor toilet in my grandfather's old vegetable garden. It's the type of set-up that makes you question the level of your urgency of need.

It's family run, just like in the movies. A mom-and-pop joint – 'Pop' doing the frying, 'Mom' taking the orders and one of the sons doing the bulk of the heavy lifting and cleaning and other jobs.

'What you folks doing round here anyway? You ain't no tourist.'

I explain I'm a foreign journalist sampling the waters ahead of the presidential election, then just a fortnight away, and ask her thoughts on the candidates. 'Oh, Trump, I guess,' she says without hesitation. 'Ain't no other choice, really,' and off she shuffles, returning to the booth a few minutes later with a fresh pot of coffee.

As she pours the steaming brown liquid into my chipped mug, commemorating in faded letters some high-school sports victory from 1987, her brow is furrowed. She's deep in thought. 'Our town ain't what it once was,' she says. 'We need help. Maybe he can bring it. He's sure done well for himself, anyway. And his family.'

It's startling how many times people mention Donald Trump's children as a qualification that he'll make a good president. It's regularly the response to questions on how voters can agree with his – at times – racist, sexist, xenophobic comments. 'I don't like that,' they'll say, 'but he's reared fantastic children so he can't be all that bad.' I've learned America is still quite a conservative place at heart. For all the bling and swagger, the American Dream, for many, means creating a good life for their children, getting them an education and a good start in life. The Trump children embody that legacy.

So it's not surprising that she mentions his children, but what is surprising is that she doesn't mention Hillary Clinton. Not once. This is supposed to be deep in Democratic country. Alarm bells should be ringing in Democratic HQ.

There are chimney stacks as far as the eye can see, but there is no activity. No smoke belching into the countryside. No steam puffing into the clouds. And there's no traffic either. It's just like a vacant film set.

This is McKees Rocks, a small town in the shadow of Pittsburgh, almost a suburb of a city known as an engine of industry. It's one of the two big cities in the state of Pennsylvania that regularly deliver this state for Democrats in presidential elections. Until 2016, it had voted for the Democratic candidate in the previous six presidential elections. Barack Obama swept to victory here in 2008 with a 10.4 per cent margin and again in 2012 with a 5.4 percentage point victory. Bill Clinton, John Kerry, Al Gore – all comfortable victors. Pennsylvania hasn't voted for a Republican since 1988, when the state went for George H.W. Bush.

At this point out from the election, the polls also show Hillary Clinton enjoying a reasonably stable lead of between 6 and 10 per cent in Pennsylvania – well beyond the margin of error of the pollsters, her campaign team assured. Donald Trump's team, meanwhile, are criss-crossing the state with appearances, double-digit visits in the three weeks before polling day.

Pennsylvania is technically a swing state, but it's a blue-leaning one. There's a political nerd joke that Pennsylvania comprises the port city of Philadelphia in the east, the industrial headquarters of Pittsburgh in the west and 'Alabama' in between. In other words, two big, liberal-leaning, densely populated Democratic cities and pure red old-school conservative Republicans in the middle. The Democratic strategy in the past has been to maximise the turnout in those big cities, so those votes outnumber the voters who turn out in the red, rural areas, thus guaranteeing an overall state win.

But traversing Pennsylvania in late October 2016, it's several hours before someone admits they're voting for Clinton.

The Allegheny River winds its way through the Appalachian region of Pennsylvania from the mines north of Pittsburgh along 325 miles to the south of the state. The Monongahela River starts in West Virginia and flows through the same area, ending in Pittsburgh. The route is entirely navigable, built to handle barges. There are lock gates and dams throughout. Rivers and railroads are the veins pumping life through this monstrous state, spanning over 46,000 square miles (117 square kilometres). It's only the thirty-third biggest state by land mass in the US. By comparison the island of Ireland is approximately 32,595 square miles (around 84,431 square kilometres).

The rivers used to be busy, filled with barges carrying steel. The slogan 'Pittsburgh built America' is true, not just a catchphrase. From the 1930s to the 1950s more than half of the steel used in America was made in Pennsylvania. The state was home to the world's largest steel-producing plant – the Homestead Works. At one point that Pittsburgh plant alone made a third of the country's steel. That's long shuttered and gone, the 430-acre site long sold. It lay desolate for almost a decade but in recent years has been transformed into a shopping centre and entertainment complex.

Once great, these rivers, and the railroads alongside them, wind through one declining town after another. When local industry was booming the politics were blue. Now that industry – and employment – remains in decline, residents are looking for hope, for change. In one bend in the River Monongahela lies Monessen.

And there, finally, I find a Clinton voter.

The woman smiles a toothless smile. Her gums are almost empty, save a few rotten stumps where teeth had once been. Her hoodie is filthy, the name of a great sporting university emblazoned across a body that has long since stopped engaging with any sporting activities. Splattered down the front are the remnants of several meals. Her tracksuit bottoms are dirty too, but she has what looked like a brand new designer handbag. Her warm heart and open face do little to disguise the ravages of a long-term addiction – possibly extreme alcoholism but most likely heroin or another opioid. 'I'm voting for Hillary,' she says proudly. 'Us women have to stick together.'

This woman is hanging around in the car park of the town's supermarket, hoping for the kindness of strangers or perhaps the pity of those who know her too long and too well. The building's exterior is almost unchanged since the day, fifty-four years ago, that President John F. Kennedy stood in this car park addressing thousands of local people ahead of the 1962 congressional and gubernatorial elections.

Everyone you meet talks about how JFK spoke here. Twice. It's like meeting a middle-aged man who was once a good footballer and still talks non-stop about that school championship he once won. The badge of honour worn with pride. This town has the frayed edges and signs of former glory just like that man with the strong shoulders and sizeable beer belly. A hint of what once was. The people here have a pride in their town, even if to a newcomer's eye it is not immediately clear that it's worth stopping in.

No man carries that pride greater than Lou Mavrakis, the mayor of this town.

He was born here. His father was an immigrant from Greece and so strong was that culture that Lou speaks with a bit of a Greek accent.

We're standing beside a coke plant – not the fizzy sugary drink, but the fuel derived from coal. The factory was built in 1942, four years after Lou was born. His father worked there, and when Lou finished high school he went to work there too. His brother, two and a half years older, went off to college.

Lou is almost misty eyed when he recalls those heady days as a young man working in the coke plant. He made more money than his college-educated brother could ever think about making, he says.

Lou worked there for nine years, then he became president of the local branch of the United Steelworkers of America (USW) trade union. Then, after another eight or nine years, he was 'promoted', he says, to the international staff of the union – looking after the interests of workers in the US, Canada, Puerto Rico and the Virgin Islands. Back then the USW had 1.7 million members. By the time Lou retired, it had fewer than 700,000.

Here in Monessen, the population is 7,483.[5] In 1940 it was over 20,250. The reason for the population decline? 'We lost 24,000 steelworkers' jobs with the exit of the steel industry,' explains Lou. 'When the steel industry left, it left us with all of this blight.'

Thirty-five commercial buildings and 400 homes are collapsing and need to be demolished. Lou and his beloved city of Monessen have no money to pull them down.

There hasn't been a steel mill here in over thirty years. The last mill to close – the Wheeling-Pittsburgh Steel Corporation plant – was used as a location for several scenes in the original *Robocop* film in 1986 but then it was closed and demolished. The extent of the town's problems were evident in the deal that was done then. The Steel Corp allowed Tobor Productions to film in the plant in exchange for a $10,000 donation to a food bank for the plant's unemployed workers – a good deal for the movie production company.[6]

The system in the US is such that a significant portion of funding for local communities comes from local tax dollars. So when a town loses population, it loses income. When it loses income, the local authority no longer has money for road repairs, for electrical faults, to keep streets clean and maintained.

And so goes the downward spiral.

'The children getting out of school today, they don't have a chance,' says Lou. 'They have to leave the community. They can't stay here. They've got to go elsewhere to get jobs and whenever you're stuck with a city like this, and you lose two-thirds of your tax base, you still have the same geographical area that you have to maintain and it makes it impossible.'

He says there are only three or four 'taverns' in the whole town now. When he worked in the plant, there were three or four bars on every block. Now he won't walk down the main street at night because it's not safe, such is the drug and crime problem that inevitably rises when poverty does. But back in the day, he says, 'You had to walk down the middle of the street because the sidewalks were full. People were all over, everybody was happy. Everybody enjoyed each other.'

Up the street, a peeling notice, tacked inside what was once a grand window: 'This building has been determined unsafe and unfit for occupancy.' This is O'Toole's Business Equipment store, a green emblazoned sign over the door, complete with shamrock design, proving the solid theory that there are Irish everywhere in the US. But not here anymore. The shop has been shut for quite a while. The lofty window display, frozen in time, features two of the latest brands of fax machine and a large, grey boxy-style PC – the kind that hasn't been top of the range and worthy of a window display for at least a decade. The shop inside is almost perfect, just like the day it was obviously abandoned in haste, save for a thick layer of dust and the obvious traces of some four-legged and tailed inhabitants.

Buildings elsewhere on this main street aren't just boarded up: they're falling down. Parts of the footpath are cordoned off because lumps of plaster and roof tiles could land upon unsuspecting passers-by at any moment.

The mayor stops every now and again to wave to a resident and exchange pleasantries or pauses to take calls about that night's council meeting. They may not have a quorum – one of the five council members has a problem getting there on time due to other commitments.

Lou is seventy-nine. He was elected mayor of Monessen when he was seventy-five. He ran as a Democrat, as he has in every election. And it's clear he cares about his town. He's anxious to show off what were once stunning buildings, with ornate cornicing and brickwork, now home to pigeons, covered in their ubiquitous grey excrement, and with crumbling corners.

He clearly cares for his community, but he's angry.

'The very communities that built this country are the ones that suffered the most.'

He's written three letters to President Barack Obama over the last year and a half. He gives me copies of the three letters. Each one articulately composed. Each one filled with emotional pleas. Each one ignored. Tearing up, he says, 'Billions of dollars go to foreign countries that hate us and yet three letters to President Obama, he never even responded to me.'

He continues, 'This country will never be defeated by a foreign power, it's being defeated from within. If ISIS were to come to Monessen, they would keep on going because they'd say somebody already bombed the damned place. Because that's what it looks like down here.'

With much of the main street fenced off, and so many falling-down structures, so many cracked, potholed pavements, it's hard to disagree with him. It does look war torn.

With what may have been blind luck or pure genius, Donald Trump picked Monessen as the location to give his first policy speech on trade. It made campaign history because it was the first time he used a teleprompter. (And why, in such a bizarre campaign, was it noteworthy that a candidate used a teleprompter? Because Trump had spent months slagging off 'traditional politicians' for using teleprompters, preferring to freewheel himself. But that led to too many cases of 'loose lip' blunders so his staff clamped down.)

And so on 28 June 2016 Donald Trump came to Monessen, to a metal recycling plant. He stood in front of bales of compacted rubbish. It was strangely beautiful and disgusting to look at, at the same time. It was symbolic – the once mighty heartland of industrial America was now reduced to a rubbish heap.

But the people here loved it.

Mayor Lou, a previously true-blue Democrat, says Trump was 'magnificent' and that he 'told the people what they wanted to hear'.

He says it's unheard of that people would be thinking of voting for a Republican in a 'Democratic bastion' where 'President Kennedy spoke twice'. But he knows it's going to happen.

Standing between the mayor and the coke plant is a railroad line. All day long, mile-long trains filled with coal go out and come back empty. Some of the coal is used to fuel coke plants like the one here in Monessen. But much of it is destined for export. Coal and coal derivatives are still the number one export in Pennsylvania, although in 2016 it only accounted for 3.4 per cent of the state's total exports. 'Just count the carriages,' says Lou.

Employing human beings in coal mines might be an outdated concept, as robots and other technologies take over, but in this part of the Rust Belt it's still a major employer, albeit a short-term one. And it's one industry where both candidates differed in the election. Hillary Clinton famously (clumsily) said, 'we're going to put a lot of coal miners and coal companies out of business'. She made the remark as part of a sentence about how she was going 'to bring economic opportunity using clean, renewable energy as the key into coal country', but it was initially and repeatedly quoted out of context, which helped to alienate a huge chunk of the voters in Pennsylvania, Ohio, West Virginia and Kentucky. Donald Trump cleverly waltzed in with 'We're going to bring back coal' – a statement that simply can't be true unless he knows a fast way to create fossil fuels.

The mayor is sanguine about it all. 'It was a bad thing for her to make a statement like that,' he says. 'She burned her bridges here in coal country. It's unfortunate. Do I believe that anybody's going to do anything for us? Absolutely not. I think they're all lying. The only way that we have a chance is they could bring some small industry back into these different areas where I'm at, but steel will never return like it used to. It's impossible. It can't happen.'

It's about three weeks out from the election at this stage, so does he think people here, lifelong Democrats who cheered for JFK as small children, will still vote for Hillary Clinton?

He sighs, like a doctor preparing to tell a patient something they don't want to say and that the patient doesn't want to hear. 'Well, these people all lost their jobs in the steel industry. And Trump is saying what they want to hear. Clinton hasn't said anything. She hasn't even come here. Several times she's been in Pittsburgh. All right, Pittsburgh is only 28 miles north-west of here.'

He says her strategy is focusing on the major urban populated areas around Pittsburgh and Philadelphia. He's correct. He rather presciently states that that's an error. There are enough people around here who've had enough and who are prepared to ignore their Democratic roots – they are prepared to ignore their better judgement about some of the offensive things about Donald Trump and are willing to take a chance.

'She's written us off. She don't even come around. And I can understand why. It's a bad situation and it's unfortunate, but the only way that anything's going to be done for communities like mine is that the government has got to come in: they've got to invest millions of dollars into our communities and get rid of the blight.'

Lou stresses again that he's a staunch Democrat and doesn't know how he'll vote. But he tells me he's so pissed off, he might just do it. He might vote for a Republican. His father would drop dead if he were alive today, he confesses. When he came from

Greece it was the Democrats and the unions that helped him make a decent living. He did it 'the right way', says Lou. He came through Ellis Island, he became a citizen, he worked his way up. He didn't expect anyone to learn Greek to help him out: 'he learned to speak American and speak English to accommodate himself'.

His next sentence suggests he favours Donald Trump and his wider platform more than he might want to admit just now. 'We've lost track of the United States. We're becoming more or less bilingual. They want you to learn to speak Spanish and speak Mexican. Come on, this is United States. Learn to speak English, that's it.'

Almost apologetically, he adds, 'I'm very frustrated.'

Then he looks right into our video camera and begs for help. 'I plead with you. This is a good place to come because the mayor of Monessen is very receptive to people coming in, bringing in your money, we have a place for you. The property is cheap here. We'll give you a property for nothing. You've got the railroad track right here, the water right over there. You've got the interstate two and a half miles away. Everything is here.'

He stops and turns to look at the trains again.

'Can you imagine how much coal is there – 113 to 120 box cars? Did you count them?' he asks.

I tell him I lost count.

'It will be 113 to 120, I guarantee. Now I understand why Hillary Clinton doesn't come here and in this area. She said she was going to get rid of coal. She made a mistake. There are a lot of coal miners, they won't forget it. Those coal miners are not going to vote for her, they're going to vote for Trump. Just stop and see how many train cars have gone by already. This happens five, six times a day, five, six times a day on the other side of the river. All coming from coal mines down south.'

He asks again how many have gone by already. About eighty, I say.

'It will be 113 to 120,' he says again.

'I believe you.'

'I've counted them numerous times, just double checking myself. You imagine how much coal?'

'A lot of coal,' I say.

'We're coming to the end now. Do you know how you can tell? You can tell by the sound. When the sound starts to die down that means it's almost over with.'

And as actual tumbleweed blows down the main street of Monessen while we're walking back to the car, it's clear that it's not just the end of the train carriages that that dying sound heralds.

It strikes me that what's happened here is not dissimilar to what happened in many parts of the UK. The anger and disillusionment here is akin to what is felt in many northern parts of England and in Wales. It can be matched closely to how the voters who opted for Brexit felt.

It's reminiscent, too, of the despondency there has been at times in parts of Ireland when big employers have closed down – Donegal when Fruit of the Loom closed, Limerick when Dell shut, Waterford when TalkTalk left. Livelihoods of generations of families were put on the line because of a corporate decision, globalisation or technological advancements.

There are differences, of course. The problems are compounded in the US due to scale – the distance to the next big town or city that could offer employment is often beyond a commutable journey – and the welfare system is almost non-existent.

But there's an argument that the lack of trust in the establishment parties is what led to huge numbers of Irish voters picking independents and new party formations in the 2016 general election, leading to a minority government. Voters were prepared to take a chance on the unknown.

That's what happened in the US, and it's well illustrated by Marlena. A local woman nipping to the supermarket to get dog food and milk, she pulls up in her car to give her tuppence worth.

Again, the first thing she tells me is about JFK. She's a Democrat; her parents were Democrats. They took her as a baby to wave a flag at President Kennedy when he came to town, a photograph that holds pride of position in her family home. But she's done with the Democrats, she says.

'Our politicians don't care. I'm voting for Trump.'

Marlena breaks down as she talks about the town where she was born and raised. Her father was a school teacher but he went to work in the steel mill because everybody did. But then it closed down and 'everybody left', she says.

'We resorted to heroin, drugs, corruption. This is like a ghost town, to a degree, but it's sad to see families being destroyed, people on welfare. That's their way of life now. There's no hope for the children. You go on the streets. What? Go buy heroin.'

She points out certain buildings. They look as derelict as many others on the main street, but with a missing door or window. They're the crack and heroin dens, she says.

Marlena went to see Trump when he came to speak in Monessen, describing it as 'an honour to do so'. Through her tears, she says she wants to take Hillary Clinton 'around the corner' and 'beat her up'. She apologises instantly. She's not into violence, she says. She's just so 'tired' and 'really upset'. Clinton, she says, 'doesn't care about anybody'. She stresses how she's been a lifelong Democrat, and voting for a Republican candidate is upsetting, but says she's now 'Trump, Trump all the way' because she wants someone who will 'go fight and save us'.

But as a lifelong Democrat, as a woman, how does she feel about some of his more controversial remarks? Particularly the boasting about sexual conquests revealed just a day or two previously on the *Access Hollywood* tapes? Her rationale is a simple one: 'Men will be men.'

'He was never a politician. He was an entertainer. He was a businessman. People change.' For Marlena, the problems are bigger. She just wants someone to fix the economy. To fix her town. She breaks down again, needlessly apologising again. 'I'm sorry. I'm angry and I'm upset.'

––––

Back up-river, a fantastic red-brick building spans one side of the railroad tracks. It looks like the sort of place that should be turned into trendy apartments or creative arts spaces or craft distilleries. But not here. Gentrification has not reached this town. In McKees Rocks, just five miles north-west of Pittsburgh, this old rail yard is crumbling. The big empty space outside, two or three football pitches in size, is full of weeds and wild flowers and all sorts of natural life. Look up from that gravel and you can see the Pittsburgh skyline, seeming little more than a stone's throw in the distance, feeling like another galaxy away.

There used to be about ten thousand people in this yard, says Taris Vrcek. He's a third-generation local resident. Sick and tired of the decline of his beloved hometown, he founded the McKees Rocks Community Development Corporation.

This was the locomotive repair facility for the Pittsburgh and Lake Erie Railroad. It employed ten thousand people on this spot and, right around it, supporting industries employed thousands more.

Taris admits it feels like a ghost town but he remembers when houses burst at the seams, such was the shortage of housing. Five large churches sprang up around the rail yard because so many immigrants flocked to the town and each wanted to worship in their native tongue.

'Vitality' is the word Taris uses for that time; 'desolation' is the one he uses for now. 'The town', he says, 'has lost its economic engine, and its heart.' They're seeing 'three or four generations deep in poverty, who are really trapped in that situation, and suffering'.

The steel heart has turned into a rust belt, and it's really rusty in this western part of Pennsylvania.

The steel industry lost 142,000 jobs between 1978 and 1998. Multiples of that in related jobs were affected too. Now, according to the Pennsylvania Steel Alliance, just over 12,000 people are employed directly in the steel industry in Pennsylvania.

'It's really weighed on this community,' says Taris. And he's clear about where he directs the blame. 'The US government has been one of the real creators of generational poverty.'

He says policies in recent years have 'eroded the work ethic' of his community. He's trying to help people there get out of generational poverty. But they're afraid, he says.

'Part of that fear comes from "I don't want to take a risk of losing my housing, losing my income",' he says, adding, 'right now we're incentivising folks not to work.' If they do go to work, he says, they lose some of the benefits they depend on to survive – not to live, just to survive.

He says this 'hopelessness' has led people into 'dangerous situations' and that many of the 'horrible things happening with police confrontations with residents' are down to that hopelessness. He says there can be all the 'law and order talk you want, it's not going to change what's happening in people's hearts and souls'.

He doesn't know how people are going to vote there. He once would have said with certainty that the Democratic candidate – whoever that was – would be a shoo-in. He can't give those guarantees this time. Furthermore, with such big problems here, he and his fellow residents are repulsed that an important contest has been reduced to name-calling during debates and general mud-slinging. 'People, frankly, are disgusted. It's an embarrassment.'

———

Donald Trump won Westmoreland County, where Monessen is located, taking 63 per cent of the vote. There are 700 registered Republicans in the town, yet 1,221 people voted for Trump. A lot of Democratic crossover; a lot in a place where everyone still talks about JFK's visits. And that's the clue: the speech President Kennedy gave in the car park of the supermarket here on 13 October 1962.

The likenesses between what President Kennedy said then and what Candidate Trump said when he came to town in June 2016 are noteworthy.

Kennedy in 1962: 'this town and other towns ... have been hard hit by all of the technological and industrial changes that have come in this country ...'

Trump in 2016: 'Skilled craftsmen and tradespeople and factory workers have seen the jobs they loved shipped thousands of miles away. Many Pennsylvania towns once thriving and humming are now in a state of total disrepair.'

Kennedy: 'How can we possibly provide for the education of our children, jobs for our people, medical care for our older citizens, better housing? Jobs! Jobs! Jobs!'

Trump: 'We are going to put American-produced steel back into the backbone of our country. This alone will create massive numbers of jobs. High-paying jobs! Good jobs!'

Maybe they're both just giving obvious political speeches, but the allusion to the hard-done-by nature of the local people and the unwavering focus on jobs worked in 1962 and it worked in 2016.

Michigan

MADE IN AMERICA!
BRING BACK THE JOBS!

Coming from the airport, before you catch a first glimpse of the skyline, you see a giant tyre – Uniroyal. That's on the left side of the highway. Shortly afterwards is a giant Ford factory on your right – just one of the forty-eight auto plants here. For this is Detroit, Michigan. Home of the big three – Ford, General Motors and Chrysler. The birthplace of the American automotive industry. The city that makes 1.5 million cars and trucks a year. Detroit: the town that keeps America driving, or so it goes. Detroit: the largest municipality to be declared bankrupt in the history of the United States, is how it is.

Although there is somewhat of a rejuvenation going on in the city centre, circling out from that you pass through a city still in decline. Boarded-up windows, shuttered-up shops. Drive north from the city and something peculiar happens. It could be to do with zoning. Locals tell me it's to do with corruption. But on one corner there's a liquor store (called Perry's – no relation) promising, in as blunt a fashion as possible, 'Fine Wines and Check Cashing'. Keep going for a block or two and the rundown look gives way to palatial vistas. Home-owners here are partial to colonnades and pillars and sun decks and water features in their driveways. And at least two have lion statues built into their welcome porches. Some houses here look like small hotels. They face the lake and, beyond that, Canada. They are ostentatious and extravagant and by and large not tacky at all. This is where The Rich live. Those who were not dramatically impacted by the bankruptcy of Detroit. Those for whom life goes on, and went on regardless. An average house price here is $306,000; in the Detroit metro area it's $39,100.

Keep going north along the Jefferson Highway and you reach St Clair Shores – clearly still a middle-class area, but not as wealthy as Grosse Pointe Shores nearer the city.

Despite the waterfront location and the connection to Henry Ford and his family, they don't get many out-of-state tourists here. Detroit has a bad name these days, and Michigan in general is considered boring. Even its licence-plate slogan is a little dull: 'Pure Michigan' – not quite 'The Empire State' of New York or 'Taxation without Representation' of Washington DC, or the 'Live Free or Die' of New Hampshire.

Not even the bona fide pop-culture street cred granted by its son Marshall Mathers, aka Eminem, seems to count for much. Here you'll find the famous 8 Mile Road, as featured in the semi-autobiographical film *8 Mile* and the song and soundtrack album of the same name. Inside Gilbert's Lodge, where Eminem worked as a line cook, there's nothing to indicate that – no plaque, no display or signed photograph. In fact, given this restaurant is themed on a hunting lodge and has a toy train running around the rafters, it strikes me as about as far from Eminem's on-screen persona as you could probably get.

Sitting at the bar, months after the election, that strange thing happens again: Irish people come out of the woodwork. The friendly bartender announces to the whole room that I'm from Ireland and I'm 'really nice'. One man shouts over to ask whether I'm carrying a knife before everyone laughs. Clearly a reference to the negative Irish stereotypes in the US, ones that, infuriatingly, we can never seem to escape. I wave my dinner knife jokingly in his direction and warn him that he'd better be careful what he says.

Then several of the friendliest barflies make their way over to me one by one to chat.

The first man is Irish, he tells me, between whiskeys. When he learns that I'm travelling around to talk about politics and the election, he says he's not interested in that. No politician ever made his life better and they never will.

The next man pulls a stuffed envelope from his pocket. His grandfather emigrated from County Clare. He's not sure of the dates. But he shows me pictures of his grandfather's brother on a trip back 'to the old country' five years ago. He visited the farm where the family had lived. Another granduncle remarkably still lives there. The thatched roof has been replaced with a tin one, and some of the outhouses are crumbling, but it's an Irish farm, and the faces smiling out are unmistakably Irish. It's one of those catch-your-breath moments. Eating yet another burger, in yet another all-American bar, and here is a man who is so proud of his Irish heritage that he's been carrying photographs around in his breast pocket for five years. He is bursting with emotion at the chance to show them to a 'real Irish-born' person. 'Doesn't it look just like a real Irish farm? You can confirm that, can't you? This is really Ireland?' Obviously, I don't know for sure where the photos were taken but the colour of the stone, the shade of green in the trees and the unmistakable light of a soft, grey Irish day leave me in no doubt, I tell him. He's delighted and proceeds to tell his grandfather's story to the whole bar.

He moves off and another man comes over. Brian is the main electrician in town. He's Irish too, he says, although he doesn't go into detail about his heritage. Things aren't as bad up here in St Clair Shores as they are in Detroit, he tells me. Everyone has jobs here. They either work in the auto plants or they make something small to sell to them – plastic clippings to hold a wire or a car part in place. Or paint. Paint is a big business.

It's a wonderful community, according to Brian, and one that proudly voted for Donald Trump. His message of economic growth, job protection and turning over the old insular political way resonated with people.

Brian was born here and has lived here all his life. He owns his 'Sparky' electrical business and sometimes does jobs for local businesses on a bartering basis. He describes a community that's almost idyllic. But nothing is protected. He tells me he lost his wife of twenty-seven years recently. To cancer. He's devastated. He doesn't want to be single. He hates being alone; but he won't look for anyone else. Nobody could compare to her. He's grateful for the health care he had – otherwise he'd be without his wife and bankrupt. (Unpaid health bills are the number one cause of bankruptcy in the us.)

Lovers of Motown, lovers of motors, lovers of modernity will all know of Detroit – it is a city rich in culture, and it is a city poor in the real sense, with crumbling infrastructure and graffiti-filled buildings, with drug addicts and dealers alternating street corners. But it is a city of hope, of rebirth, home to a people who've seen glory days and will again. The global headquarters of General Motors is here – in the aptly named Renaissance Building. These are people who cheered along with Barack Obama, witnessed his bailout of the auto industry, who ached for change, who saw their city bankrupt and bailed out and had to start again. And then who voted for Trump.

Candidate Donald Trump came to the Freedom Hill amphitheatre in Macomb County on the Sunday night before election day. In that final week, he did two Michigan rallies, returning time and again to shore up support.

But he wasn't the only one. The Clinton campaign did the same, and on the day before the election Hillary Clinton held a rally in Grand Rapids, Michigan, and she sent her second-best surrogate, Barack Obama (second only to his wife Michelle), to Ann Arbor in Michigan.

Lifelong auto worker Chris Vitale went along to one of Trump's rallies. He'd long since decided he was going against the leadership of his union, the United Auto Workers of America (UAW), who had endorsed Hillary Clinton.

'I'm actually a believer in unionism, but that doesn't mean I'm a believer in the president of the UAW,' he says.

He feels that the Trump campaign team never thought they could win Michigan. 'They didn't even have a campaign machine. They had, like, three campaign offices in the state and this is a big state. None of them were local. It was like they thought, "Oh, the unions are going to vote Democrat and we're not going to win these people over." But I talked to their people and I said, "You can win this state, just deliver," and I wasn't the only person saying that.'

Chris didn't go to the final Trump rally, even though it was on his doorstep – partially because he knew he was going to vote for him anyway, but more so because of the potential traffic jam.

'I was doing some work in the garage, had the radio on, and I heard them come on with a traffic report. I had never heard them on a traffic report just say, "Do not go anywhere near these mile roads or these intersections, certainly not 16 and Schoenherr." And that was before the rally. Traffic was at a stand still. They just couldn't find room to park people. They were so packed out, people started just parking along the road and it turned into a street party.'

What Chris seems to think was inevitable does not seem to have been made widely known to the Clinton campaign. But the two local papers in the area – the *Detroit Free Press* and the *Detroit News* – both printed articles in the days before the elections screaming 'Danger Here'.

Five weeks out from the election, it was said to be all but over in Michigan, with a decisive victory for Clinton. She had an eleven-point lead across the state, a thirty-point lead in the rock-solid Democratic stronghold of the greater Detroit region and tradition on her side. The last victorious Republican candidate in the state was George H.W. Bush in 1988. Since then, every Democratic candidate had won in Michigan, regardless of whether they won the overall election. But the *Detroit Free Press* poll a few days before election day had her lead cut to four percentage points. Most polls come with a warning that their margin of error is plus or minus three percentage points, so a lead of four points is quite literally a marginal lead and not anything you'd want to use to bet the house on. Her lead among women had dropped from twenty points to eleven, and the thirty-point lead in the Detroit metro area had been halved, not least due to a predicted low Democratic vote in Macomb County. That prediction came true. Having twice plumped for Barack Obama, with a margin of 8 per cent in 2008 and 4 per cent in 2012, this time Macomb County went for Donald Trump. With a winning margin of 11.5 per cent, it was a whopping turnaround.

That fifteen-percentage-point turnaround Trump victory in Macomb County is largely what won the state of Michigan for him. In that district just north of downtown Detroit, Donald Trump got 48,351 more votes than Hillary Clinton, but statewide in Michigan his winning margin was merely 13,107.

It's a little early to say 'as goes Macomb County, as goes Michigan, so goes the country', but the pattern is there.

That's the county Chris Vitale works, lives and votes in. He says he was predicting his county would flip for Trump for months, and he was fairly certain the state would too. Easy to say in hindsight, except Chris appears to really have his finger on the pulse. He's a third-generation auto worker and an elected county official. In St Clair Shores – where he's a councilman – it's so egalitarian they're not permitted to be registered members of any party; they have to just serve the people.

Chris voted for Barack Obama in 2008 – 'only because he was the lesser of two evils' – but by 2012 he was so annoyed with him, and things in Detroit were taking such a dark turn, that he wanted to make a point. He didn't want to vote for the Republican candidate, Mitt Romney, then – 'he was terrible … very dismissive, very arrogant' – but 'there was no way I was voting for Obama either. I voted for the third party Libertarian candidate whose name I couldn't tell you if you put a gun to my head. I don't even remember who it was. It could have been Mickey Mouse. I always vote.' (The 2012 Libertarian candidate was Gary Johnson – he made it onto the ballot in forty-eight states plus the District of Columbia, with write-in status in Michigan, which is how Chris was able to vote for him. Oklahoma was the only state where voters could not pick Johnson.)

Before Chris Vitale came over to Team Trump, he was going to do the same this year and vote for Johnson again. He knew he could not and would not vote for Hillary Clinton because it was 'more of the same', and by this stage he had a deeply engrained hatred of Barack Obama, but neither was he going to vote for Donald Trump, initially viewing him as 'another clown getting in the race'. He watched him on *The Apprentice* occasionally, but that was 'the corniest thing I ever saw. I realised all he really did was pop on the show for five minutes in the beginning, five minutes at the e..d and he probably filmed it all on the same day. I never really took it seriously.'

When Trump got in the race, Chris initially thought it was a Hillary Clinton 'distraction' tactic. He was plumping for the Republican senator from Pennsylvania, Rick Santorum, at that stage of the primary contest, before Donald Trump had emerged as the party's nominee. Santorum had finished second in the race to be declared the Republican Party's nominee in 2012.

So why Santorum? He doesn't have the liberal viewpoints that Barack Obama has or that Chris's 2012 pick Gary Johnson had.

'Initially because Rick Santorum comes from Pennsylvania. It's a steel-producing state. He was one of the sole Republican votes against NAFTA [North Atlantic Free Trade Agreement]. He has been outspoken on trade, to his credit, and I identified with some of his other positions. Initially, I was a Rick Santorum guy, but I also knew in the back of my mind that he'd run before, hadn't made the cut. He would be attacked because Rick Santorum … well, he looks like the whitest guy you've ever seen. He was like Captain Country Club, Captain Glee Club. I've never heard anyone say a bad word about him, even Democrats, so he's a very wholesome guy. But I also know wholesome guys get beat up, spit out and thrown away. Even though I liked him, I really didn't think he'd probably make it to the finish line.' Indeed, Santorum didn't make it to the finish line to be declared the Republican party's nominee.

Enter stage-right, please, Mr Donald J. Trump.

Chris remembers the speech Trump made when he descended those gilded escalators in Trump Tower in June 2015 to announce his plans to run for the White House. 'He made a very controversial speech that was supposed to sink him, where he talks about "Mexico isn't sending us our best people."'

The exact quote from Donald Trump is: 'When Mexico sends its people, they're not sending their best … They're not sending you [the crowd of his supporters gathered in the lobby of Trump Tower]. They're sending people that have lots of problems, and they're bringing those problems with them. They're bringing drugs. They're bringing crime. They're rapists. And some, I assume, are good people.'

Chris says that speech made him think back to an old boss he had when he used to work in Arizona. He was there from 1999 to 2003 and his boss was Mexican born, 'one of the nicest bosses I ever had, loved the guy'.

He says they were talking about immigration one day, a frequent topic of conversation in Arizona as it has a sizeable immigrant population, given it is a border state. One in six people in Arizona is an immigrant, either with or without paperwork. One in five of those living in the state is Mexican born.

Chris says his Mexican-born boss shocked him at the time.

'He said, "You know, Chris, you should know that people that are coming over the border, those are like the worst Mexicans. Those are like the ones – think about it, they up and leave, run across the border. They don't have any roots in their community or anything like that. A lot of them have got warrants and things like that." He was essentially sort of trying to explain away to me the idea ... I think what he was trying to say is that, "You shouldn't think all Mexicans are just a bunch of border jumpers," which I didn't necessarily think that. I knew that that wasn't the truth. I worked with Mexican engineers out there and all kinds of people, but he felt the need to tell me that. He said almost word for word what Donald Trump was saying. I think he even said something like, "The worst people come over; well, not all of them."'

So when Chris heard Donald Trump speak, 'It just grabbed me, like – that's what your old boss used to say!'

Then he started listening to him more. And then he just knew.

'I heard him talking about how this country's trade policies are negotiated by a bunch of bureaucratic hacks and political appointees; that they're terrible at negotiation. When he says that they're political appointees and hacks, he is 100 per cent right. Those people, when they go in there, they know they're going to have that job for four years at the least and eight years at the most, because the next administration is going to come in and blow them out of there. They make nice beds, little feather beds for themselves to lie down in when they're gone. That is really a nuanced understanding. Even though ... Most people don't know that. Even though he talks in these big terms, and he says "hacks and crooks" and whatever, he understands a point of this that the average person, or the above-average intelligence person, doesn't even know unless they really understand how these people make and why they make these policies.'

But, ultimately, what matters to Mr Vitale is NAFTA.

Chris says pretty much every one of Donald Trump's promises is something he agrees with.

'I pay for government to do some core functions: protect the borders, negotiate trade deals, pave the roads, these sort of things. I see that almost none of these things are getting done. Infrastructure is falling apart. Borders have become a joke. Trade deals are a payoff.'

This was the difference for him in picking Donald Trump over Hillary Clinton. 'Why in the world would I vote for somebody that's going to keep that slow march to the slaughter line going? Even if he's a guy that blows up the system, then blow it up.'

To many voters from countries like Ireland with a popular vote system, the US electoral-college system is hard to understand. It doesn't seem fair that a small number of voters in a swing state like Michigan could have more value than thousands or even millions in a state like California or New York. Donald Trump was the legitimate winner, but it can be hard to process that more individual voters picked Hillary Clinton than picked the victor.

Chris Vitale is one of the few people I've met who describes himself as a fan of the electoral-college system. His logic is simple: 'I don't think you can have 300 million people governed by people in three cities. That's a recipe for disaster. Some guy in Idaho is going to get told how he's going to run his life by somebody that lives in LA?' His theory is that the electoral-college system protects the rural people, those not living in the big, liberal cities, so that their voices can be represented alongside the city folk.

Chris is a bright guy. He works hard. He's writing a book. He has a hobby refurbishing vintage cars. He has friends around the world and takes an interest in global affairs.

Statistically, Trump won the election by winning a majority of white men with lower levels of education, fulfilling the stereotype of the Trump voter as an angry, ill-informed, ignorant white man.

    This 'kills' Chris, he says. 'The other stereotype of the Trump
voter is that they're not real bright, and they don't think things
through, and they're afraid, they're xenophobic, they're afraid of
people from other countries and things like that. First of all, my
wife's been to Ireland twice. I've been to Germany. One of the
reasons I know so much about these policies in other countries is
because with the Internet, the advent of the Internet, I have friends
all over the world.'

    What's interesting about Chris is that he's a staunch union
guy, a member of the UAW. At its peak in 1979 that union had 1.5
million members – a substantial voting bloc. It's not as influential
as it once was, but its active and retired membership now totals
just over a million people; 412,000 of those are actively employed
autoworkers.

    The president of that union, Denis Williams, endorsed
Hillary Clinton in May 2016, saying the Democratic candidate
'understands our issues on trade, understands the complexities
of multinational economies and supports American workers,
their families and communities'. The statement continued, 'she
also works to support good-paying manufacturing jobs here in
the US by opposing the Trans-Pacific Partnership, and recognizes
the need to address unfair, existing trade agreements that weaken
American manufacturing jobs'.

    But here, Chris Vitale says, 'the United Auto Workers
management could not be any further removed from the workers
on the factory floor'.

    The UAW did a survey in September 2016 that showed one in
four union members actually supported Donald Trump – not a
majority, but enough.

    As with the pattern witnessed in other developed economies
in recent years, unions are weakening here. In December 2012
Governor Rick Synder signed a right-to-work bill into law. That
meant from then on there was no longer a legal requirement for

workers to join a union before taking up a contract of employment. Chris says that some people resigned from the UAW once the law came into force.

The Democratic Party is known nowadays as the party of the worker, the pro-union party. With the UAW, as Chris Vitale puts it, 'the support always goes to the Democrats'.

But that wasn't the case this year for him. So although the President Dennis Williams called on all members to vote for Hillary Clinton, he didn't. He sees union leadership as being too political, too focused on fundraising. He was telling people at Chrysler to vote for Trump, he knows another man who works at Ford who was doing the same and he's pretty sure somebody in General Motors was doing something similar.

One of Donald Trump's core messages is that of Americanism, 'America First' – 'buy American and hire American'. At rallies and speeches, he talks favourably about his love for the 'Made in America' label. Although Chris Vitale is the third generation of his family working in American manufacturing, he believes that message is xenophobic and doesn't account for the foreign companies in the US who are employing Americans making non-American products. Of which there are plenty. In a major study undertaken by the Brookings Institution in 2014, 5.6 million Americans were employed by foreign-owned entities. From an Irish perspective, 700 Irish companies with operations in the US employ 800,000 people here. When it comes to manufacturing, 18.5 per cent of Americans working in that sector were working in foreign-owned companies in 2011, the most recent statistics available. So pushing a 'buy American' mantra means not purchasing the products made by those 18.5 per cent. If you follow that logic through to its natural conclusion, that means a lot more unemployment.

Chris does wish Trump had explained the 'America First' slogan a little, as he knows it puts off people in other countries, when actually it shouldn't.

'I wish he would have added to that America first, Britain first, France first, Ireland first – all these countries should begin putting the interests of the people that elect them to office first. That's where you get honesty.' The way Chris sees it, if he has a president that he voted for who isn't willing to put America's interests first, then there is a big problem.

Does Chris Vitale think people like him and his co-workers helped to swing Michigan for Donald Trump? 'Most definitely.' He says that most people working in the auto industry in the state are actually quite conservative. The Democratic message doesn't necessarily 'line up with who we are here'.

Bernie Sanders won the Democratic primary in Michigan, but Chris is not a fan of his either. 'Most people here don't work a forty-hour week, they work a sixty-hour week,' and through overtime that put them into a bracket where they would end up paying more tax under Bernie Sanders's plans – not an attractive option for anyone. He only won the Democratic primary contest, says Chris, 'because people couldn't stand Hillary Clinton'.

They 'connected the dots' between her husband, Bill, signing the NAFTA legislation and the loss of manufacturing jobs, meaning the loss of tax dollars in the area. That led to the decline and bankruptcy of Detroit and now is resulting in the decline of Flint, the neighbouring city.

Chris is completely opposed to NAFTA. It is the single issue that drives most of his ire against the established political network and attracts him to Donald Trump.

At this stage, we know that Donald Trump is opposed to trade deals. On his third day in office he withdrew the US from the Trans-Pacific Partnership agreement that his predecessor had signed up to. He also has pledged to renegotiate NAFTA. But there haven't been too many other details.

And Chris admits that he's 'cutting him quite a bit of slack' because, 'honestly, nothing that Trump has said has been really nuanced or very refined on the idea of trade policy'. But for him the point is that Donald Trump is talking about it. He's talking about it in a way that appeals to Chris Vitale and his friends.

'I remember when we were sold NAFTA. I was twenty years old, and I paid attention politically at twenty. I remember being sold NAFTA as the idea that we were going to create this Mexican middle class that was going to buy all of our products.'

But that hasn't worked out.

'First of all, they're relatively small markets compared to the US. I think they're probably not even a fifth of the size in terms of volume. The other thing is, they can't afford to buy very much because their average middle-class manufacturing wage in Mexico is so low. All we did was just find another place to exploit labour. We didn't create a middle class.'

He blames NAFTA for the difficulties the car industry has experienced and the problems his own city and state has had too, leading to Detroit becoming the largest US city to declare bankruptcy.

He also thinks there's a direct correlation between NAFTA and the problems of Flint, Michigan, some seventy miles north-west of St Clair Shores.

'You have this hollowed-out shell of a city with 50 per cent of the population, not far off from what happened to Detroit, and they can't afford to pay their bills. Their system falls apart. Their infrastructure falls apart. They have to make stupid choices, like hooking up to a river and not adjusting the pH levels so that you strip all the fluoride off the pipes and start leaching in lead. That's what happened.'

Then President Barack Obama travelled to Flint, Michigan in May 2016, drinking a glass of filtered Flint water on live television to show things were getting better, acknowledging the situation had been a 'screw-up', and it had been.

In April 2013, looking to save money, Flint city officials decided to switch from the supply managed by the Detroit Water and

Sewage Department to the Karegnondi Water Authority supply. Upon receiving notice of the end of the contract, Detroit told Flint they had one year to switch over and they would turn off the supply in April 2014. As that deadline loomed, it was clear to Flint that the pipeline to the KWA supply would not be operational on time, and as an 'interim' measure they decided to take the water from the Flint River.

By May residents were complaining about the smell and colour of the water. By August E. coli and total coliform bacteria had been detected in the water, and by October General Motors announced it was going to stop using Flint River water in its factories. It feared the water would cause corrosion in its machines. Flint authorities had not taken action to immediately treat the water, which was high in chlorine, to ensure it didn't damage the pipe network.

By January 2015, the Centre for Disease Control found that Flint was in breach of the Safe Drinking Water Act because 'disinfection byproducts' were found in the water. This occurs when chlorine interacts with organic matter in the water creating total trihalomethanes, or TTHM.

In February, the local Michigan public radio station reported that water with high lead levels was being detected in residents' water supply. In one woman's home the lead content measurement was 104 parts per billion. The Environmental Protection Agency (EPA) says the safe limit is 15 parts per billion. Independent researchers from Virginia Tech University did a test later and found lead levels in the woman's home to be at 13,500 parts per billion. The EPA considers water with a lead content of more than 5,000 parts per billion to be 'hazardous waste'. The lowest level of lead in the water samples taken by the Virginia Tech researchers was 200 parts per billion. The World Health Organisation maximum allowed level is 10 parts per billion, and the EPA's 'action level' is 15 parts per billion.

This essentially toxic substance was being piped into this woman's home to drink, cook, wash and bathe her children with, all to save money for the city, a city struggling in the aftermath of globalisation and technological developments.

That woman is LeeAnne Walters. She was the first brave resident to draw attention to the water supply in a city that much of the world had forgotten about, where 40 per cent of the population, in a majority black city, live below the poverty line. She started speaking up and then shouting up when she noticed the water coming out of her tap had an orange hue. Then she noticed her twin boys had rashes. Then doctors confirmed one of the boys was showing signs of stunted growth.

Ms Walters has four children. One son, aged five, may have potentially irreversible lead poisoning. It took eleven months from the first suspected water test result before the EPA issued an emergency water notice in Flint.

LeeAnne Walters testified before the US House Oversight Committee in Washington DC on 3 February 2016. She is articulate and captivating, but what she had to say to anyone who would listen is shocking.

'My home used to be a place of comfort and safety for my family. It used to be what a home should be: a place of peace and protection from the outside world. That was taken from us, and not just from my family, but from every home and every citizen in Flint. Now my home is known as Ground Zero … We now know the horror of poison running through our taps and the negligence of the agencies paid to protect us.

'My children are dealing with health issues. The one with the lead poisoning has a compromised immune system. He's only gained 3.5 pounds in the last year. He's still dealing with the anaemia and he has developed speech issues.

'We need to make sure that the children and all of the people in Flint are taken care of health wise. I know my children are going to need help with that. I know other children in the city are going to need help with that and not just the children under the age of six. I know of a fifteen-year-old who has severe liver issues now, who has lead poisoning. A forty-four-year-old man who had an eye stroke because of problems with his blood pressure with his lead poisoning. So doing right for the people is going to be making sure we're taken care of and making sure we get clean water, get the pipes replaced, once we have the science behind it to see exactly what we need to do to get the replacement done.'

This became an election issue. A favourite refrain that Trump used time and again on the campaign trail was 'It used to be cars were made in Flint and you couldn't drink the water in Mexico; now the cars are made in Mexico and you can't drink the water in Flint.'

While this may just seem like a catchy slogan, it was a brilliant message for the people in Flint and across Michigan. People who had seen their city and state go from an economic powerhouse to bankrupt before their very eyes. People who had seen prosperous times morph into an era where the water was poisonous because the authorities had to try and save money wherever possible. Here was Trump talking to them about the issues that mattered to them. They had been left to fight bureaucracy on their own. One mother had to go to Washington for help and to plead for the situation to be resolved. The people felt let down by the Democrats, desperate, in need of action.

According to Chris, 'It's funny to me, the idea that we're worried about Trump because he has essentially a resort business. He has hotels and golf courses. He's not an armament maker. He's not a chemical company. He's not any of these things that could really have the potential for harm. If a whole bunch of people from other countries book a Trump hotel, is it likely to cause the end of the world?'

His wealth is appealing to voters around here too, says Chris. 'They look at Donald Trump as though he has what we call "F-you money". He's so rich, he doesn't have to care. His kids will live the rest of their lives without having to work. He doesn't really have to be bought.'

And what about those Hollywood tapes with Trump boasting of his conquests with women? Chris is brutally honest about that.

'There's an element in people that says what he's basically talking about is the kind of woman that's going to throw herself at him because he's rich. There a lot of people that know that's true. There are, unfortunately, a lot of women who do that. Now, granted, he didn't express that very eloquently. He didn't sound like he really had a problem with it, but I think people actually looked at it and they were like, "Oh, this guy's not afraid to call a spade a spade." It's not the way I would have said it or something like that, but … I think the idea was that he's not aware that he's being recorded, obviously. This is intended as a bombshell, to bring him down. I think people felt like, "That's the worst we're going to hear, that he says these horrible things, that some percentage of us knows that there's some basis in reality for this?" Let's face it, a lot of women trade on their looks, but you know what? A lot of men trade on the idea that they can dunk a basketball. They're not rocket scientists either, and we know that. I think a lot of people just looked at that like, "If this is the worst thing I catch him saying, and he doesn't even know he's being recorded, then I can probably live with that."'

This is one of the more honest, articulate and slightly terrifying justifications I've heard for those Trump comments, which were generally slammed by Republicans and Democrats, men and women. A sort of 'ah well, everyone does it so it's grand' attitude. Should leaders not be held to a higher standard? Should heads of states not be people that you would hold up as a model of what one should aim to be like, not an example of the average person, with limited respect for women?

But Chris counters that, while he 'says dirty talk and nasty things', 'he's not supporting a certain culture', and has hired many women in his businesses. And as for not releasing his tax returns: 'Does it bother me? Not really, because I am, in addition to working at Chrysler and in addition to being on city council, I've always been a hustler. I have rental properties and things like that. One of my buildings, I've been trying to sell it, can't sell it. Real-estate market's gone down the toilet. I've come to realise that it's actually better that I just take a loss on that building, and not sell it. I'm not going to give it away – I'll put it that way. I'm not going to give it away, because the fact that I'm having to make the payments and everything on that, without any income coming from it, negates a lot of the taxes I'd have to pay making money on the other properties. Trump is somebody who knows what tax laws are and uses them to his advantage. So what? Now, I'm not on the same scale as Donald Trump, of course.'

Chris is basically answering the broader question of what Donald Trump, a man born into wealth who used that wealth and privileged position to generate more wealth, has in common with people who work hard for a living. And it's just that – he's an everyman. Despite his station in life, he still talks trash, he likes to make a quick buck and he has no problem using the system to his advantage. All things that Chris says he and most others do too.

But Chris is really annoyed about how divided the country is right now. That to him is the biggest failing of the US at the moment. 'Eventually, we're going to have to get down to business. We can have all these protests, and we can have all these court proceedings and things like that, but eventually, people are going to run out of appeals, and they're going to run out of the energy to go out there and protest this, because I don't know any person with a job that has time to go out. I support Donald Trump, but I didn't blow a day off work to go to his rallies. I guess they're what we call the silent majority, that just goes to work every day and tries to do what we've got to do.'

But despite all his hopes for Trump and for America under Trump, he thinks most people don't really care and would prefer 'to sit home and watch *Dancing with the Stars* instead'.

And then there's immigration. Michigan admitted more Syrian refugees last year than any other state apart from California – although that was just over 1,300 individuals, a minuscule amount in a state with a population of 9.9 million people (according to the 2014 US census).

Dearborn, Michigan, a suburb of Detroit, is home to the largest mosque in North America. Nearby Hamtramck has the first majority Muslim city council in the US.

Chris Vitale has an interesting take on immigration – on this he isn't quite aligned with Donald Trump. His grandfather fled Sicily when the family ended up on the wrong side of the local mafioso. Chris is proud of the Italian Sicilian culture in his family, but he considers himself an American. He likes Italian food, but he knows that the Italian food he cooks and eats in the US is not like the original. He admits that's because 'we Americans love to put cheese everywhere' and he probably wouldn't really like the authentic meals served in Sicily. He points out how Irish Americans have traditions that Irish people do not (St 'Patty's' Day being an example – as poor old St Patrick spins in his grave). But Chris feels this is the true beauty of America. Immigrants bring their cultures here and they merge them into something American and that's how it should be. A mish-mash, a melting pot. But those new cultures should still be welcome to come, he says. He feels that is not a message that Donald Trump puts across.

And maybe it's because he has spent most of his life looking across at another country. At Canada, another great landmass within swimming distance of Detroit, separated by a river. A shiny bridge goes from Detroit to Windsor, Canada. There are no heavily armed guards on the shores, no border-patrol boats zigzagging the water. The situation could not be more different at the other end of the US, where another river separates the US from Mexico.

Texas

BUILD THE WALL! BUILD THE WALL!

There are shell casings in the undergrowth. Lots of them. Not yet covered up by vegetation. Not yet rusted by exposure to the elements. Fresh ones. There is a flip-flop stuck in the mud. Just one. Where is the other one? Where is its owner?

This is Texas. Well, more specifically, this is the edge of the United States. The bank of the Rio Grande. The border with Mexico. Standing here at one of the narrowest parts of the at-times-mighty river, it looks maybe just 20 feet wide. Definitely a wade-able distance.

It's approaching dusk and we've been warned not to be around here after dark. It's not safe, the local border police had said. Especially for two very pale, white Irish people driving in an obviously brand new, and quite large, rental SUV.

We'd wanted to get some footage of the Rio Grande to use in our story for RTÉ News about the US–Mexico border – to show just how narrow the river is at parts and to see the locations where Donald Trump wants to build a border wall. A lot of the riverbank here around McAllen, Texas is private property or is heavily fenced off. Finding a good vantage point was proving a challenge. Spotting a border-patrol car in the parking lot of a Burger King off the highway, we'd pulled in and asked the officer waiting on his burger and chips where he would recommend. He gave directions, which we thought we'd followed, and ended up driving down a dirt track to where we found ourselves now.

This was not something worth getting shot for, so with the light fading, and conscious of the warnings from the locals, we decided to get back in the car and return to civilisation. Too late. Two car headlights pierced the twilight between us and the main road. They were moving at speed. In our direction.

The dirt track was only wide enough for one vehicle so we had no choice but to stay where we were. As the lights approached, they were blinding and made it hard to tell what type of vehicle it was. However, it was unlikely that any 'coyotes' (people smugglers) would be using such a bright light. Correct assumption. It was border patrol. But that did not mean they were friendly. We knew we were innocent, if naive. They did not.

They approached us with weapons fully drawn and set their aim straight at us.

'Do not make any sudden movements. Do not get out of the vehicle. Keep your hands where we can see them,' one officer yelled at us.

A second and third vehicle arrived on the scene. More border guards. More guns. I had to remind myself that this was the United States and not a war zone. We had rights. They wouldn't just shoot us. Or would they? Except it is a kind of war zone here. The authorities face a nightly battle against heavily armed, extremely dangerous criminal gangs that traffic drugs, guns and illegal immigrants.

As the officers approached us, their demeanour appeared to relax a little. Could I have imagined it was because they saw that we were white? Possibly. Would things have been different if we had a black or brown skin tone? Probably. There are enough disturbing videos on social media to show how badly wrong things can go when police officers yell at you not to make any sudden movements – or sometimes don't even give that warning.

'What are you doing here? This is private farmland. You should not be here after dark.'

We explained who we were, showed media credentials, showed passports, showed visas.

Perhaps they are used to sophisticated criminal gangs with well-thought-out cover stories, because they sure weren't buying ours. The team leader radioed for his superior and for the canine unit. More vehicles. More guns. Big dogs.

The commanding officer arrived and grilled us further. They asked us to get out of the car extremely slowly and walk towards their vehicles, while the officers opened all of our luggage and gear bags and the dogs searched the car.

The superior eventually decided to let us go, warning that he could have brought us in for further questioning, but he seemed satisfied that we were in the wrong place at the wrong time, that we had just taken the wrong turn off the highway.

All of the officers were polite at all times. But their resources are stretched. Our presence had been detected by a heat sensor and verified by a drone. The size of the vehicle had caused them concern. They'd checked with the landowner to see if he knew us, and when he didn't, protocol dictated the full response effort be deployed.

Chris Cabrera is a border-control guard working in the Rio Grande Valley. He's stationed with the Customs and Border Protection Unit in McAllen. His colleagues were the ones we 'encountered' that evening.

His job is a tough one. There aren't enough agents and he says the border itself is 'far from secure'. The US–Mexico border itself is 3,201 kilometres, or 1,989 miles, long.

'It's never been fully secure and it seems, as time goes on and things progress, we get less and less secure with each passing day.'

Chris is a big, fit guy, with tight-cut dark hair, of Hispanic origin – like many people in this part of Texas. This did, after all, used to be Mexico.

Looking back on that part of us–Mexico history through a modern prism is fascinating. President James Polk from North Carolina became president in 1845, elected on an express platform of expanding us territory and taking land from other nations to declare it part of the United States. This was mostly done by violent means – not unlike some modern-day world leaders who spring to mind.

The us–Mexican War, which ended on 2 February 1848, was a battle over the Republic of Texas. It ended with the signing of the Treaty of Guadalupe-Hidalgo, which established official borders between the us and Mexico, with Mexico ceding Texas to the us.

The us also essentially seized control of northern Mexico, which then included California, Nevada, Utah, New Mexico and Arizona, along with parts of Wyoming and Colorado. They were reimbursed by President Polk for the land – the princely sum of $15 million. In signing the treaty, Mexico lost over half of its landmass.

Back on the modern-day Texas–Mexico border, Chris Cabrera describes the job of a border-patrol agent. 'Well, how it's supposed to be is that we're out there in the brush, in the wooded areas between the ports of entry, whether it's right on the river in some areas or right on the international boundary, and either preventing people from entering or apprehending people as they enter along with a contraband, whether it's drugs or whatever the case may be.'

But that's not what has been happening of late.

'What happens now a lot of times is large groups of women and children are turning themselves in to the agents, so the agents are having to congregate in that area to take these people into custody.' In other words, sucking up their already stretched resources.

'Meanwhile,' he says, 'the bad guys, the really bad guys, the criminals that know they're not … they won't be able to get any type of asylum, they're coming in around the sides. It's like a bait-and-switch type of deal. They know that the smugglers know when to send these women and children to us because they know we're going to have to take care of them, and then all the people are coming right around the side with guns, drugs and money. Whatever the case may be, they're coming in right along the side.'

So what's the bigger problem along the US–Mexico border: illegal immigration or contraband – the drugs and guns?

'I think it's both. We have a lot of drugs coming in. We have a lot of guns going south to Mexico.' What, wait? Illegal smuggling goes south? Out of the US into Mexico? Yes, of course it does, but you would not pick that up from listening to President Trump. The US is the innocent party, suffering at the hands of those he describes as 'bad hombres'.

But Chris Cabrera says any border agent will tell you it's a two-way street. 'Any time you have drugs and guns, that creates a very dangerous environment, whether it's to the average citizen or to law enforcement on any level, so that's a big problem.'

However he does agree with President Trump on something surprising. He feels bad on a humanitarian level for those who are seeking a better life in America, but he says not all of those fleeing from Central America are as innocent as you might think.

'We have people that are convicted felons, that are murderers, rapists, child molesters, burglars. We don't need those people coming in. If we were to apprehend one of those, chances are they know they're going to jail for a long time, so, usually, at those points, it becomes a more difficult situation because they do have something big to lose.'

This is Agent Carbrera's nuanced way of saying when they intercept the wrong type of illegal immigrant, that's when gun battles break out. Those individuals know they'll be going to prison, or swiftly deported if arrested, and killed if they return to their home countries, so they might as well take the risk of dying now or firing on the agents and getting away.

Chris is also the spokesperson for the National Border Patrol Council, a trade union/employment organisation for the agents.

They were one of the first labour groups to officially endorse Donald Trump during the 2016 campaign.

And while Chris himself appreciates the support he and his co-workers are receiving from the attention the president is directing their way, he does not think a wall is the answer.

'I don't agree with it … I mean, I think a wall or a fence, it is a good thing, but not in and of itself. It can't stand alone. It'll never stand alone. You look at the White House. They have a fence, but then they also have people patrolling the fence. They also have ground sensors. They also have cameras, so even they know that a fence works, but not alone. I think there is good talk about it. The thing that Mr Trump brought to the table has made people talk about border security as opposed to any other election year where we were just lost in the shuffle. To me, it's my job, and I think it's very important. We need something to secure this border, whether it's a wall in conjunction with manpower and other resources.'

There is already a fence along about a third of the border. It is high. It looks like the kind you would see outside a prison complex. It runs across people's land. At various points you'll see people chatting through it, passing things to each other – on occasion, crying and hugging through it where a deported person is on one side and their relatives on the other. It doesn't seem imposing, though. More of an eyesore. More intimidating are the powerful weapons that the border-patrol agents carry on their person, attached to some of their vehicles and positioned on the back of the boats that patrol the Rio Grande itself.

Agent Cabrera explains about the fence.

'They put them up close to residential areas or more urban areas so that people wouldn't run into the neighbourhoods and then you have car chases and people running all over the place. It makes things dangerous. The problem is we put those sections up and we thought, "Well, now, they're secured," so we concentrated on the outlying areas and they just came right over the top. Any fence we ever built, they've either gone over it, under it and, sometimes, through it. Unless you have manpower securing that fence in addition to the wall or a fence or whatever you want to call it, it just won't work.'

Sitting in his windowless office with flickering overhead fluorescent lights, it feels far removed from the core job of a border-patrol agent. 'A wall in and of itself is not going to fix anything. Once, they put up sections of the wall down here, they put an eighteen-foot fence up, the next day, we had nineteen-foot ladders right up against the fence. The biggest thing is the agents. You need more agents. You need agents allowed to do their job and do what they know how to do, because a wall by itself or a camera is not going to be able to put hands on anybody and arrest them, so we need to get those agents in there.'

So wearing his hat as vice-president of the National Border Patrol Council, how many more agents would it take to make things more secure?

'I don't think we need too much. It may be 1,000, 2,000, 2,500, somewhere in there. But I think the big thing is we need to let our agents be agents instead of babysitting. Instead of dealing with some of these humanitarian issues, all the processing that goes with it, let our agents be out in the field and work. Let us do our job. We're probably the only union you've ever heard of that is asking for more work. Most people are trying to get out of it. Hey, let us get in there. Let us do our job. Let us secure the border because that's what we know how to do.'

Agent Cabrera feels things are getting worse, though the number of people crossing illegally has tapered off from the recent high of 414,397 in 2014. That was a particularly bad year, as there was a crisis in terms of the number of unaccompanied children crossing. Some 68,541 children made the journey across the Rio Grande that year. In the year to the end of January 2017, over 25,000 unaccompanied children had crossed into the US along the southwest border. The majority came from El Salvador, followed by Guatemala, then Honduras, then Mexico. In the year to the end of September 2016, a total of over 408,000 people had been apprehended at the border with Mexico. Official figures from US Border Patrol also recorded 322 deaths. Most of the apprehensions, and sadly most of the deaths, happened around McAllen, here in the Rio Grande Valley.[7]

However, when listening to President Trump talking about the large numbers of people 'flooding' across the border from Mexico, it is worth remembering that in the year 2000 over 1.6 million people crossed illegally into the US at the Mexican border – more than four times the number that crossed last year. So while it is still a significant number, it does not compare to the numbers that were crossing at the end of the Bill Clinton presidency.

But according to Agent Cabrera, the pressure and the stretched resources are starting to take their toll on agents.

'Unfortunately, we're seeing more people dead. Whether they're drowning or from the elements – it gets pretty hot out here and then we have the snakes that go with it, so we're starting to see more of that. On top of that, our hands are tied. We're not allowed to do our job the way we do it. We bring people in, and 80 per cent of them we have to release them to go further into the country. That's just not the way we're designed.'

He's talking here about the 'catch-and-release' scheme, which has been the solution to the problem caused in recent years by more people crossing the southwest border than there are places in detention facilities and a backlog in the immigration courts. The US authorities literally have no way of coping with the numbers of people coming over the border.

The last leg of the journey for genuine immigrants, who have trekked through forests and across mountains, is to swim, paddle or wade across the Rio Grande. Then they sit and wait for the border-patrol guards to find them. They're brought to a processing centre in one of the towns – in this case, McAllen has its own processing centre. Here the immigrants, the men, women and children, can be split up and families separated. It is distressing, but they are at least in America, sleeping in a building with a roof rather than out in the elements as they may have been for the previous three weeks or more. Once they are processed, if they can provide an address for a responsible guardian, a relation who is in the US legally, they are given the price of the bus fare to get them there and a case number. Then they are 'released', as Agent Cabrera puts it, and Uncle Sam essentially pays for them to 'disappear' into the middle of America. The case number will eventually result in a hearing date at their local immigration centre. However, the backlog is such that the waiting time is usually several years. While some do make it to court, by that stage many have vanished into the shadows – either purposely or because they've moved on from that initial 'responsible guardian' address.

'We need to stop this catch-and-release system. We have people coming in, turning themselves in, and we're releasing them further into the country for an undetermined amount of time until they can see a judge, which is four, five, six years away, so more people are coming. We're releasing them, and it's just compounding daily.'

He is under no doubt that that system is what is encouraging people to come.

'Now, they know they can get released, people are coming in. They're getting released and they're calling home. They're putting it on social media that they got released and more people are coming. They know it's a guarantee if they can turn themselves in to a border-patrol agent, say a certain keyword – that they're in fear for their life or in fear for their safety – that we will let them stay and, unfortunately, more and more people are doing it. We're seeing 400, 500, 600 people turn themselves in in a day.'

Out of sight of agents, the fence looks ultimately scalable, if you were so inclined and possessed a certain skill set. The river, though, is just so narrow in parts. For example, Anzalduas Park is on the US side of the Rio Grande in McAllen, one of dozens of parks and wildlife conservation areas on the border, a really beautiful area. It has picnic tables and barbecue areas, large green spaces for family kick-abouts and a landing dock for border-patrol agents. Directly across the river on the Mexican side is the Centro Cultural y Recreativo La Playita, a similar park and picnic area. Both sides are well kept. Both sides are popular family spots. You can wave across at people on the other side and with a loud enough voice a conversation would be possible. And so immigrants swim or wade across the river and climb up on to that landing dock where the water-bound agents do their shift change or meet for an iced tea. The immigrants just hand themselves in. No drama. No chase.

That is the pattern that has annoyed Agent Cabrera and his colleagues, fuelling them to endorse Donald Trump at an early stage. They don't wish ill on those genuinely in search of the American Dream, but they do resent the process. As he explained already, he wants to be out there 'catching the bad guys' and not processing humanitarian cases. That is not an efficient use of his skill set, and truthfully, he is right. He is a highly trained and highly skilled law-enforcement officer; when resources are so thin already, and so many criminal gangs are active on the border, filling out forms seems like a task that could be given to civilians.

He really wants to see the system reformed and the border secured. 'I think both need to be done, but in order to do the reform, you have to secure the border first. It's like if your sink were to overflow with water, do you start mopping the floor first or do you turn off the water? Most people would turn off the water, and that's securing the source, and then after that you mop.'

He is not happy either about those who hire illegal immigrants – a welcome workforce in this part of the US where farm labourers and ranch hands are always needed, jobs many American-born people snub their noses at.

'There has to be something done with people that are hiring these folks as they come in because if we continue to give them an incentive to come, they're going to continue to come. Who wouldn't come? They're going to continue making this journey. Some people don't make it through. Some people die along this journey. It's a very difficult journey. Whether it's on humanitarian level or national security level, either way, that border needs to be secured to save lives.'

Chris is not automatically a Republican. He tells me his 'roots' are Democratic and 'the conservative side is coming from our job', but he voted for Donald Trump. He says he made the decision based on 'what's good for my job, what's good for my family, what's good for my country'. His sister voted for Trump too, but only because he was the Republican and she's a 'straight ticket Republican'.

Chris Cabrera's hesitancy about the border wall is not unique. Survey after survey of the people living in these border regions shows a population opposed to its construction. In general, about two-thirds are opposed to building the wall, but that becomes higher the nearer you get to the border.

Even President Trump's first Secretary of the Department of Homeland Security, and subsequent Chief of Staff, John Kelly, isn't in favour of it. During his Senate confirmation hearing, he gave a variation of Agent Cabrera's 'If you build it, they will scale it' argument when he said, 'A physical barrier in and of itself – certainly as a military person that understands defence and defences – a physical barrier in and of itself will not do the job. It has to be really a layered defence. If you were to build a wall from the Pacific to the Gulf of Mexico, you'd still have to back that wall up with patrolling by human beings, by sensors, by observation devices.'

_____

Evidence of the human flow over the border can be seen in its most raw form across town at the Sacred Heart Catholic church in downtown McAllen.

It's Tuesday afternoon and every half an hour or so volunteers erupt into applause as the latest busload of newly arrived illegal or undocumented immigrants arrives. This is the next stage in that catch-and-release system Agent Cabrera mentioned. Once the new arrivals have been processed by the authorities in McAllen, they come to the Sacred Heart Catholic church to wait for their bus journey to Vermont or Maryland or Kansas or Washington State, or wherever their relatives are.

There are few more emotional places in the world than the community centre at the back of the Sacred Heart Catholic church. This is community action in its purest form.

As a structure, the hall itself is like any parish hall anywhere. Taped lines on the ground mark out a basketball court. Colourful scenes are painted on the wall. In one corner there is a makeshift creche, with tiny tots playing with colourful toys. The fixtures and fittings have probably seen better days, but there have always been better causes to fundraise for other than the hall itself.

But that is where the similarities end.

Along one wall, an eighty-five-year-old woman has used bingo tables to make a long rectangular shape. It's covered with soap and shampoo bottles, feminine sanitary products, toothbrushes and toothpaste, baby lotions, nappies, deodorants and a host of other toiletries. She comes every day and is in charge of rationing these precious commodities to the weary travellers who have most likely not seen a shower, bath or possibly even a sink for weeks. She also keeps control of plasters and bandages and cough bottles, throat lozenges and over-the-counter painkillers. They are like gold dust here. The journey is not an easy one and many arrive with colds and flus and chills from exposure to the elements.

In the centre of the hall are about ten circular clothes rails. They're filled with clothes organised according to size and age, with men's clothes on the left, women's on the right. Along the other wall cubbyhole-style shelving holds shoes, running shoes and boots. Many of the immigrants arrive in flip-flops; some are barefoot. Apart from the poverty element, they're coming from warm countries and many have never worn anything other than a sandal or similar sun-shoe. They need shoes badly, and those making journeys north need footwear that can withstand the cold.

At the back of the hall is another room, which has been turned into an industrial kitchen, churning out meals to the ravenous. The local restaurants continuously send food donations to the kitchen. On days like today, when more people have come over the border than usual, there is a danger they'll run out of food. The manager has made a quick run around some local restaurants – could they spare anything? The local Japanese restaurant sent two large plastic basins – almost the size of laundry baskets – full of steamed rice. That causes great excitement. It is filling for the new arrivals, and it will go far. They sent vats of stir-fried vegetables too. More smiles from the volunteer staff, something nutritious to offer. Meat is rare, but that's OK. The plainer the food the better, say the volunteers. The immigrants come from different food cultures and may not have eaten much recently. Giving them food their systems are not used to generally makes matters worse.

I was literally left holding a baby for about fifty minutes here. One of the volunteers had been holding him while the baby's mother filled in some forms. Then the volunteer needed to attend to something and I was the nearest pair of available arms so the baby was passed to me. I had no idea if the mother was in the room or, indeed, if she was watching me. Was she watching this blonde white woman in a nice dress cooing, rocking and attempting to sing Spanish-language lullabies to her most adorable, soft bundle with deep brown eyes? Yes, I could have gobbled him up, but it would have taken a hard heart not to feel the same way. This baby, about three or four months old, had been carried in swaddling clothes on his mother's back for a month – about a quarter of his life – and now he was in America. The land of opportunity. The land of the free and the home of the brave. Now he could do anything, he could be anything. His life expectancy immediately improved.

Eventually his mother came back. A young woman. A very young woman. She had gone for a shower and something to eat and a fresh change of clothes. The chance to do that by herself in peace for half an hour was too good for her to resist. Any new mother anywhere knows the joy, in those early weeks and months, of an uninterrupted shower and the chance to wolf some food down and put some clothes on that aren't milk splattered, to sit down quietly for a few minutes as waves of exhaustion wash over you. This young woman was no different. Except she had been sleeping outdoors for three or four weeks. And even that was better than the violence she had escaped in El Salvador. Through her shyness and my rusty Spanish we managed to have a conversation. She expressed her gratitude and I my good wishes. And then she was gone. Off to the bus station to catch the first in a series of buses that would take her to a distant relative in New Hampshire. I wondered how she would cope. By the time she reached New Hampshire there would be snow on the ground. A lot of it. And a cold temperature that she would never have felt in her life before.

There has been much debate in the US about Syrian refugees and how this country simply is not pulling its weight in the world order when it comes to opening its doors to those fleeing unbearable violence. It was a problem during the Obama administration, and with President Trump's early attempts to ban Syrian refugees indefinitely, it's an even greater problem now. But the US is a long way from Syria. It has a significant number of displaced persons who need shelter arriving daily on its south-western border, and it does not handle that well as it is.

The words of Emma Lazarus's sonnet 'The New Colossus' inscribed on a plaque at the Statue of Liberty come to mind standing in the middle of this parish hall, as wave after wave of vulnerable but hopeful, exhausted and anxious fellow human beings arrive – for most, their worldly possessions are now simply the old and dirty clothes they're wearing.

> Give me your tired, your poor,
> Your huddled masses yearning to breathe free,
> The wretched refuse of your teeming shore.
> Send these, the homeless, tempest-tost to me,
> I lift my lamp beside the golden door!

These people are tired, poor, homeless; they are huddled together here awaiting the offer of a new life in the US. But the elephant in the room is that once they leave and get on those buses, they will disappear into what is somewhat poetically called 'the shadows' – living without the correct paperwork, looking over their shoulders constantly, hoping they're not unlucky enough to be caught in a deportation raid or for running a red light.

In the middle of the Sacred Heart parish hall, lifting up her lamp beside the golden door, is Sr Norma Pimentel, director of the Catholic Charities of the Rio Grande Valley. Today over 300 people came across the border and arrived at the hall in dribs and drabs. Usually they only see about fifty people. She leads the applause as each new minibus arrives from the Immigration and Customs Enforcement (ICE) Center. That's where the immigrants go once the border-patrol agents have intercepted them.

'They've been through so much and their countries are that kind of type of welcoming country. When you go to their country, you're a stranger and you go visit them, they will applaud for you. So we felt we can applaud for them as well because for the very first time, as they are here in the United States, they're having a chance to be welcomed. To say, "You matter to us. You're a human being. You're a person, and we want to help you." So they feel wonderful.'

Sister Norma speaks with almost Spanish-accented English. But she is Texan born, from Brownsville right on the edge of the US–Mexico border at the Gulf of Mexico. She has lived most of her life on the border, frequently speaking Spanish, so it's almost as if English is her second language and not her mother tongue.

She started this makeshift shelter operation in the summer of 2014 but is quick to point out that it was a whole community effort. Apart from a surge immediately before the US presidential election in 2016, when the smugglers, the coyotes, were warning people to get to America before Donald Trump was elected, 2014 was the last big crisis point. The immigration authorities were releasing parents and children into the bus station to wait on buses to their relations.

Sister Norma remembers it well.

'We had hundreds of people at the bus station that needed help. They were dirty, muddy, hungry. They were in great need of medical attention. Most of the children were dehydrated, and so the community responded with wanting to help them because you saw a mother and infant, and they needed help. It's natural to view as a mother, see another mother in those conditions, you want to give them food. They want to give them milk, everything that a mom needs. So that was the response of the people here in the valley, especially here in the community of McAllen. So when they started to do that, it became very chaotic at the bus station. Imagine trying to operate a bus station with so many people and people taking food, taking clothing, taking this and that. It was chaos, and so I received a call that said, "Help us." So immediately I took the lead to organise that humanitarian response that was already in the hearts of everybody here in the community. So I borrowed this parish hall and I asked the priest here, "Please let me borrow it for a couple of days." And we're still here way over two years later.'

This Catholic nun, in her sixties, has a kind and open face. When the immigrants arrive they are hunched over, cautious and fearful. But after a few moments in her company, they are smiling and relaxed. After a while they too join in the applause for the latest busload of arrivals, people newer than they are.

The scene outside the parish hall looks like a refugee camp in the Middle East. Three large army-surplus-style tents with benches are lined up in rows outside. The tents have fans inside, and as is the preference of the Texas natives, they offer shelter from the searing heat and burning sun. But for the new arrivals it's too cold inside the tents – they prefer to sit outside in the heat that they are used to. Air conditioning is not standard issue in Guatemala, El Salvador or Honduras, where most hail from. One women says the immigration centre was a *caja de hielo* – an icebox. She spent the night there and, in light T-shirts and leggings, her children were freezing. She thought this was some sort of torture. A volunteer explained it was just the standard air-conditioning temperature.

But these are the lucky ones, as hard as that may be to believe. Commander Daniel Walden knows all about those who don't end up in border-patrol custody.

———

Commander Walden is part of the volunteer reserve unit of the Brooks County Sheriff's Office and founder of the Texas Border Brotherhood. The name itself conjures up notions of vigilantism but that is the opposite of what it stands for. It's a group of volunteer law-enforcement officers for whom care and salvation are the objectives.

By day, Walden is a senior sergeant in the Donna, Texas police department, where he also works as an instructor for other law-enforcement officials in how to deal with human trafficking.

Outside of that, he and a group of fourteen reserve deputies in Brooks County assist law-enforcement officers in tracking immigrants and chasing human traffickers. This county is the poorest in Texas. It's not actually on the border but is far enough away (75 miles) that it's often where immigrants first surface, either in search of water or because they have a designated meeting spot there.

He offers to bring us on a two-hour drive through Brooks County, showing us the 'landmarks' of the US–Mexico border immigration story. There's a rest stop where immigrants come into the county, concealed in vehicles until that point. Brooks County is the only place I've encountered in the US where there is a US-passport border control tens of miles from the actual border to check that you are who say you are and that you don't have illegal immigrants hidden in your vehicle.

Walden also says there are several abandoned homes he and his fellow 'brothers' regularly check because he has found unaccompanied minors there who have made the harrowing journey alone, or who have been dumped there by the traffickers who had promised to bring them to a safe house but instead abandoned them just over the border.

Sadly, Commander Walden has also found many dead bodies of those immigrants hoping for a better life but who succumbed to dehydration or exhaustion or some other ailment they'd picked up on the course of the journey. Most of the county is rural ranch land, and if immigrants stray from the main roads, either to keep a low profile or in search of somewhere to shelter for the night, they often get lost and then they don't make it. Walden says he found over forty dead bodies in 2016.

There are some horror stories of militia groups patrolling the border and shooting on sight anyone they suspect is an immigrant. Texas is an open carry state, which means if you have a legally held firearm you can carry it in the open – a handgun strapped to your belt, a shotgun slung across your shoulder. The opposite status is a state with concealed carry laws; this means your firearm is legal but should not be visible to the naked eye.

When Donald Trump talks about building a wall along the US–Mexico border, his comments are usually focused on Mexicans. But most of those crossing are not from Mexico. In fact, current US immigration policy states that Mexican immigrants are turned around and deported immediately. It is the ones from third countries, like Guatemala, El Salvador, Honduras, who've travelled to the US–Mexican border, who avail of the catch-and-release system. People like Evelín and her two children, a fourteen-year-old daughter and an eight-year-old son. They sit in that makeshift shelter in that community centre in the Catholic church in McAllen, glad there is no wall yet. People smugglers are using the prospect of its construction as a scare tactic, to encourage immigrants to pay their passage and go now if they are considering emigrating to the US.

Evelín told me about the several thousand dollars she had to borrow to pay these smugglers who set them on their journey. Leaving her husband, the children's father, behind, the little family walked for twenty-four days from El Salvador. Leaving this community centre, they all got on a bus to travel to the east coast to her own mother. A mother she hadn't seen for five years. But getting to the US, getting into the system, waiting for a deportation hearing, that's only the beginning.

Donald Trump comfortably won the state of Texas and its sizeable pot of thirty-eight electoral-college votes. However, he won by a far narrower margin than Mitt Romney did in 2012. Romney beat Obama by a margin of 15.8 percentage points; Trump only beat Clinton by a margin of 9.

Although Texas is now a firm red state, its major cities are blue – Houston, Austin, Dallas, El Paso and San Antonio all preferred Clinton.

Of the thirteen counties in Texas that have a border with Mexico, Trump only secured a victory in three, which is a stark statement on the desire for a border wall among those who will actually have to live with it.

Florida

PLEASE USE THE FRONT DOOR

The coffee on Calle Ocho in Miami is the best in America. It's not just hot, brown water served by the pint: it's small and dark and potent and bitter, like proper blow-your-mind-open-and-set-you-up-for-the-day coffee should be. Calle Ocho is in Little Havana, so *maybe* the coffee is Cuban, smuggled in large amounts to avoid the import ban or brought one package at a time in the suitcases of those who return to Cuba for holidays. Either way, the leathered old man who serves it is giving nothing away.

'De dónde es el café?' I ask. 'De Cuba? Es verdad?'

He just grins back at me, saying if I like the coffee, I should really try a mojito – they're even better. I'd love to sink into a tall, cool glass of limey, minty deliciousness but it's only 10 a.m. so still a little early for hard liquor.

He looks at me like I'm insane. Why would I refuse a mojito? I assume that when you get to his age, it's never too early for a mojito or a margarita or whatever you bloody well want.

Calle Ocho is a magical place. You turn a corner and suddenly the ostentatious, sybaritic elements of Miami fade away and you're in a place truly worthy of the definition of an ethnic enclave. If you've no Spanish here, you're not communicating. Full stop.

Miami is simply like no other place on earth, let alone like anywhere else in the US. Cultures and peoples blend as easily as the cocktails do. There's Little Havana, Little Haiti and surrounding areas, both full of immigrants. Nowadays they're not strictly from either Cuba or Haiti but from a hotchpotch of Central and Latin American countries and islands. Then you have the über-wealthy in areas like Coral Gables. Then the young, party-loving types on Miami Beach, with the expressly beautiful and wealthy on South Beach.

My friendly señor at the bar is still pushing a mojito. I must look like I need one. I opt for another cafécito (a tiny but super-sweet Cuban espresso). I'll be wired for the day. Others come and go for a colada, which contains several shots in one cup to be shared around, or a cortadito – much like an Italian macchiato, an espresso with some foamed milk on top.

I'm in the Cubaocho Museum and Performing Arts Center. It's packed with all sorts of art – paintings, sculptures and other items which could possibly be high art but could also be bric-a-brac to the uncultured, uneducated eye.

There are mismatched chairs and tables inside, upstairs and downstairs, and spilling onto the pavement outside. It has a funky, eclectic vibe. It is a polished, Americanised version of the bars and cafes in Old Havana itself.

There is plenty of talk of politics among the old Cubanos here on this Monday morning, but even though the election is approaching, none of the debate relates to that. It's all about their old country.

Immigration is a concern, but it's always been a concern. The bigger deal is the Obama-led US normalisation of relations with Cuba, welcomed by younger people here, rejected by the older members of the community. Resuming diplomatic relations is one thing, but real change will come if, or when, Congress lifts the trade embargo.

But the 2016 campaign was so divisive and personality driven that there wasn't much room for substantive policy discussions.

The three presidential debates at times descended into rough talk and name-calling. The 'Cuba situation' was barely mentioned. Most are still not clear where Donald Trump stands on the matter.

Occasionally at Trump rallies throughout the 2016 campaign you would see a 'Latinos for Trump' poster. They weren't a completely rare sighting, but they were few and far between. However, Trump managed to grab 29 per cent nationally of the Latino/Hispanic vote. In Florida, he fared slightly better, finishing with 34 per cent of the Latino vote. It was clearly not the majority, but for a candidate who spoke with such determination about blocking illegal immigration[8], and with such ferocious negativity about Mexican and other Hispanic immigrants, it is perhaps remarkable.

However, it would also seem that Democrats grossly miscalculated by assuming that because of Trump's position they had the Latino vote sewn up. It was, to be fair, a justified calculation. After all, Barack Obama had won 67 per cent of the Latino/Hispanic vote in 2008 and a record-breaking 75 per cent in 2012. The Democratic Party in recent times has been seen as the multicultural party, the liberal party, the party of newcomers, the party of all races and ethnicities. However, the miscalculation arose – perhaps – from the assumption that immigrants or immigrant communities would stick with that party once they settled into the country and put down roots. However, on paper, the Republican Party more closely aligns with the philosophy and culture of some Latin American populations. They are mostly quite religious and conservative. Look how popular the Catholic Church is, for example, in Latin America, compared to Europe or the US itself. It is no coincidence that the current pope is Argentine. And many Latino populations are vehemently opposed to abortion – to the point that, for many, that could be the deciding factor in how they voted. These populations could also be said to value the family unit above all else, rate highly the ability to work hard and better oneself – a sort of self-determination – and look down on those who do not have a work ethic and rely on welfare. They are also in search of the elusive American Dream, improving one's lot through education and elbow grease.

On Biscayne Boulevard in Miami, some young Cuban American artists have painted an elaborate wall mural. It depicts a drift of pink pigs with wings on their backs flying through a clear blue sky. The pig at the front of the drift is wearing a blue suit jacket, white shirt and red tie, but has the face and hair of Donald Trump. Written to the side of illustration are the words 'When Pigs Fly'. Gihan Berera, from the group of artists calling themselves the New Florida Majority, explained the reasoning for the mural. 'We're having a Trump roast', he said at the time of painting. 'It's crazy to imagine that Trump with his vulgarity could become president. That could only happen when pigs fly. That's the only way that could happen. Then we realised, "Shoot, that could happen." And we wanted to get people involved.' So they did, but clearly to little avail.

Could it be said that the Latino voters handed any states to Trump? Probably not. However, given how narrow the margins were in some of the states that ultimately gave him his victory, every vote counted. So while there were few 'Latinos for Trump' signs at rallies, there clearly was a significant portion who formed part of his 'silent majority'. So why would they have voted for him? Why did they not stick with Hillary Clinton and the Democratic Party?

Almost one in five eligible voters in Florida is Latino, the fifth-biggest immigrant population share in the US. Only the border states have a higher percentage of immigrant voters – New Mexico has the highest percentage of Latin voters, followed by Texas, California, Arizona and then Florida.

According to the 2014 American Community Survey of the US Census Bureau, the Latino population in Florida totals 4.79

million, about 24 per cent of the total Florida population, and of those about 53.4 per cent are eligible to vote. Nationally, Latinos make up 17.3 per cent of the total US population, and overall, 46.1 per cent of the Latino population across the US is eligible to vote. There are approximately 57 million Hispanics in the US, and it's the country's fastest growing demographic group. About two-thirds of the grouping were born in the United States. Although it is understandably hard to quantify the total number of undocumented immigrants in the US, it is estimated that there are about 11 million and that 78 per cent of them are from Latin America.

Mark Hugo Lopez, the director of Hispanic Research at the Pew Research Center, has been asking why Latino voters opted for Donald Trump. He surveyed members of the Hispanic community and the population as a whole after the election and before the inauguration. The findings give further credence as to why Democrats should not have so wholeheartedly relied on Latino voters. Hispanics say immigration is only number five on their list of priorities to consider when choosing a candidate – roughly the same value given to that topic by the US population as a whole. In other words, it is not the number one issue, which may have been what campaigners thought. The number one priority for Hispanic voters for the Trump administration and Congress to deal with is education, followed by defending the country from terror attacks and strengthening the economy. Fourth place goes to reducing healthcare costs, and then comes immigration. So Hispanic voters put their families' welfare, prosperity and financial security ahead of other issues. In other words, they are no different to non-Hispanic voters.

When surveyors asked Hispanic voters what sort of president Donald Trump would be after the election, 50 per cent said he would be either great, good or average, and 40 per cent said he would be poor or terrible. That's broadly in line with the population as a whole, where 38 per cent of all Americans thought he would make a poor or terrible president and 53 per cent said he would be good or great.

If further evidence was needed that Hispanic voters are not necessarily a class apart and do not need necessarily need 'special targeted messaging', just look again at the Pew Research Center's findings when Latino adults were asked what they thought of the Obama administration. The statistics show that Latino voters helped secure nationwide victories for Obama, as they did here in Florida in 2012 and 2008. However, by the end of his eight years, while more thought favourably of him than compared with the population as a whole, 36 per cent still felt his failures outweighed his successes. And as we know from many surveys and interviews, rightly or wrongly, Hillary Clinton was perceived as so similar to Obama that her reign was being referred to as President Obama's third term.

But Obama had won Florida by the narrowest of margins. During the 2016 campaign, Michelle Obama was reasonably frequently referred to as Hillary Clinton's 'secret weapon'. There is no doubt she was the spunkiest stump speaker on the team. Her position as first lady, above politics per se, meant she could roll up her sleeves and deliver verbal right and left hooks without reproach. She was fond of reminding voters at rallies, particularly in the final weeks, how her husband had won Florida in 2012 by an average of just thirteen votes per precinct. That is an incredibly thin margin. As in Wisconsin, Michigan and Pennsylvania, votes in Florida matter. Not all votes are created equally in the United States.

It's easy to say the Latino vote is crucial in Florida, but the state is still two-thirds white. If Latino voters have the same concerns and motivations as the population as a whole, it is difficult to target them. It used to be that older Cubans were Republican and many of them deeply resented Barack Obama's move towards the normalisation of relations with Cuba. But Cuban Americans, the younger generation, do not hold those same deep-seated beliefs.

However, a look at the exit polling in Florida from the 2016 presidential election shows that those of Cuban descent were around twice as likely as Latinos of non-Cuban background to vote for Donald Trump. The majority of Cuban Americans in Florida voted for Trump; no other Latino demographic in the country did that, the majority voting for Hillary Clinton. Donald Trump won the state with just a margin of 1.2 per cent.

Two-thirds of Cubans who are eligible to vote in America live in the greater Miami region. It's an area with three main city hubs – Miami, Fort Lauderdale and West Palm Beach. Did the Cubans of Miami give Trump the state of Florida – and in doing so give him a big leg up to win the overall contest?

There is no exit poll data of Cuban Latino voters from the presidential elections in 2008 and 2012 to compare to the 2016 exit poll data. However, surveys consistently show a shift towards the Democratic Party, away from the strong commitment to the Republican Party which was the traditional Cuban Latino alignment.

That in itself is another reason why the polls were not as reliable as in past elections. There is an acceptance now that many of them are skewed in a way that does not easily capture Latino Hispanic voters – for example, often the pollsters don't speak Spanish and so can't account for those without a good command of English, or because a higher proportion of Latino voters have lower-paid, shift-oriented jobs, they are not always available to answer at the time the polling companies call.

The exit poll data that shows such fervent support for Donald Trump among Cuban Latinos in Florida is not delineated by age, so making exact judgements is dangerous. However, anecdotes and personal experience show that it tends to be the older Cubanos who favour Trump. They fled Fidel Castro's Cuba during the revolution in the 1960s and are now in their seventies. They rejected the Democratic Party, feeling betrayed by JFK's behaviour in the Bay of Pigs, and were won over by President Reagan – especially sightings of him wearing the famous Cuban guayabera (a uniquely Cuban man's long-sleeved shirt, cut long and loose, with four pockets for your cigars, pens, wallet, and 'ostras cositas' – the other little things that men may want to carry around. Really special ones are made with Irish linen and can cost up to four hundred dollars).

When Reagan became president in 1981, he re-imposed the travel ban to Cuba and toughened economic sanctions. He later put Cuba on the state sponsors of terrorism list. He also started Radio Martí, named after the Cuban writer and national hero José Martí (later a television station followed). This was paid for by the US government but broadcast into Cuba. Initially it was located in Washington DC, but later moved to Miami. It served to broadcast anti-communist messages and information to Cubans, and it was welcomed by those who had fled Cuba. Its first broadcast was in 1985 but it is still on air today and can be caught online as well as on the original shortwave radio frequency.

Just as Donald Trump made a push for the so-called 'Reagan Democrats' across the country, he also targeted Reagan-supporting Cuban Americans in Florida. Three weeks before the election date, then President Barack Obama relaxed even further the embargo on Cuban products by allowing American tourists to bring back unlimited quantities of Cuban rum and cigars. That was perhaps an ill-timed reminder to those who did not favour the normalisation of relations that the system would likely become even more lax under a President Hillary Clinton. In addition, Donald Trump scheduled a rally with veterans of the failed Bay of Pigs invasion. He accused Obama and Clinton of 'helping' the Cuban regime.

Back in 1999, toying with a run for the White House, Donald Trump addressed the Cuban American National Foundation in Miami. He joked that when Cuba was free he would open the first hotel there, and then went on to mention the large crowds there to hear him speak and how it was supposed to be just 100 people but 'thousands' had turned up and there were 'lines that are waiting outside to get into the room'. Fast forward to October 2016, and he was saying the same thing.

Speaking to those Cubans in Miami in 1999, he said what the room wanted to hear: 'I've had a lot of offers to go into business in Cuba … and I've rejected them on the basis that I will go when Cuba is free … Putting money into and investing in Cuba right now doesn't go to the people of Cuba: it goes into the pockets of Fidel Castro. He's a murderer, he's a killer, he's a bad guy in every respect and frankly the embargo against Cuba must stand.'

Coming back just two weeks before polling day may have been seen as a desperate attempt to shore up a certain portion of the vote in Florida, always a swing state but looking swingier than usual in 2016 because of the high proportion of Latino voters.

His hard line was just the antidote to the Clinton policies of continued normalisation. Even if Clinton had wanted to sail her own boat, President Obama's decision to further relax rules so close to polling day would have reinvigorated all those old anti-JFK, anti-Democratic feelings. Just as the announcement that healthcare policies would be rocketing made a few weeks before the election undoubtedly hurt Clinton on a grand scale nationally, so too did this announcement among certain strata in the Cuban community. It is puzzling why the Obama administration didn't more closely consider holding off on this announcement. The polls at that point in Florida were just giving Clinton a narrow lead and such a controversial issue was bound to have sway. Perhaps they calculated that it would sway in the right direction, or perhaps they were so confident of a Clinton victory that it didn't matter to them.

That veterans' group in Little Havana – the Bay of Pigs Association – ultimately endorsed Donald Trump, and as an opinion piece in the *Miami Herald* newspaper had predicted on

2 November, six days before polling, Donald Trump won Florida and Cuban Americans likely helped him to do so.

The thaw in relations with Cuba is one of President Obama's signature foreign-policy achievements. It is one of the most significant developments in US foreign policy for some time. It is intended to be life-changing for those in Cuba, and when I visited there just nine months after the first moves to normalise relations, a more positive feeling was already in the air. However, the move was not universally welcomed.

Julio González-Rebull flew combat and resupply missions aboard a B-26 bomber during the Bay of Pigs invasion. He told reporters in 2014, when he was aged seventy-eight, that he felt the Cubans had been betrayed by two US presidents. First was JFK, who made the decision to invade Cuba and then failed to provide promised air support, leading to the deaths of nearly 120 and the capture of around 1,200 of the invaders. The second president to betray them was Barack Obama, not necessarily for seeking to normalise relations, but for not seeking enough in return – namely the resignation and removal of the Castro brothers. And Hillary Clinton suffered by association.

But can Trump's victory in Miami be put entirely down to Cuban Americans? Of course not. But as we are dealing with such small margins, every point is relevant. And it is worth noting that the Hispanic tide of support the Democrats were banking on did not surface.

———

As Florida is a state with such large ethnic populations, immigration in general was always going to be a hot-button issue. According to the latest US census figures, there are about 450,000 unauthorised immigrants in the Miami–Fort Lauderdale–West Palm Beach metro area alone.

While some communities favour large numbers of immigrants – needed to do the jobs that many Americans won't do, like low-paid hospitality sector work, or jobs they've no interest in, like farm-labouring – other communities feel this 'cheap labour' is driving them out of business and should be shut down. But statistics show that immigrants make up only 17 per cent of the total civilian labour force and unauthorised immigrants account for 5 per cent of that, and they are mostly employed in construction and service jobs.[9]

Larry and Harry Williams are identical twins. They live in Miami. In their early sixties, they have deep Florida tans and snow-white hair and moustaches. They used to have a labouring business in Miami but, as Larry puts it, 'We watched our business disintegrate, because the labour force came in and we couldn't compete with illegal aliens. They just took over working so cheap.' They desperately want to see a clampdown on unauthorised workers and support Trump's stance on this. 'I think he'll have more control over the country. He takes a hard stand on it. He's a business man. He realises the problems.'

His brother Harry agrees. 'I think building a wall will be good for us. Every country in the world has got borders that separate us up.'

There is another interesting phenomenon with the immigrant voting populations, particularly those who are just first- or second-generation American born, and it's not unique to Florida. It's a phenomenon that was witnessed in Boston and New York when the first wave of Irish immigrants arrived in the late nineteenth century too. And that is a propensity to pull the ladder up behind them. The early waves of immigrants arrived and had to bob and weave and rely on luck and hard work to attain a certain station in life. Then the authorities 'catch up' and things become more difficult, and those who are unauthorised can cause difficulties for those already there. It does not mean that the more settled immigrants are mean-spirited or racist. They just feel, often, that they did it the hard way and so should everybody else. There should be no shortcuts, or as it was often said, 'no jumping to the front of the line' and 'no coming in the back door'.

This point was raised by former President Barack Obama in his first public appearance since leaving office in spring 2017, when he was speaking to young people at the University of Chicago. He urged them not to assume that 'everybody who is against the current immigration system is automatically racist'. He reminded them that the 'history of our immigration system has always been a little bit haphazard, a little bit loose, a little bit determined by "did the country want more workers", economic imperatives, sometimes driven by biases. If you look at what was said about the Irish when they were coming in the wake of the potato famine, they talked about them in the same way you hear people talking about immigrants today. This is an example of everybody being able to see the reality of immigrants as people not just like "some other".'

Among white communities, the anti-immigrant backlash can be in some part attributed to a fear of too much change – a fear that the racial make-up of their neighbourhood, their state, is changing. It was a fear that Donald Trump tapped into. Sociological statisticians have predicted that white people will be in the minority in the US by 2040. That is questionable in itself, as there is a wider sociological question of how people of mixed race identify themselves. But the statistic is often quoted by conservatives, especially those using it to prove an anti-immigrant point. Last year was the first that more non-white babies than white babies were born in the US. One in five marriages in the US is now a mixed-race marriage – another statistic used to foster that fear of immigrants. Donald Trump, with his strong position on keeping immigrants out and deporting those already here, spoke to those fears. Although 'building the wall' would have no impact in Florida, the message was welcomed.

The United States is a country where racism is a present concern – it was not buried with the successes of the civil-rights movement over fifty years ago. Live here for any considered period of time and the undercurrent of racism is plain to see. Statistics bear it out too, particularly in terms of how much more likely you are to get a degree and have a higher salary if you are white, and how much more likely you are to be a single parent or end up in jail if you are black.

But a study by the Pew Research Centre released in May 2017 lays out that fear of immigrants for the world to see. Nearly half of those surveyed said the numbers of immigrants should be decreased. Half said immigrants were making the economy worse and increasing crime. The views differed dramatically when it came to the racial make-up of immigrants. Nearly half of all Americans had positive views of Asian immigrants (who now account for the largest share of new immigrants); 44 per cent had a positive view of European immigrants. But only a quarter of those surveyed had a positive view of Latin American immigrants (26 per cent) or African immigrants (26 per cent). Break that down in terms of the political preferences of those surveyed and the results match the 2016 election exit polls and the anecdotal tales: 82 per cent of Democrats or Democratic-leaning independents think immigrants strengthen the US; only 39 per cent of Republicans do. Asked specifically if they viewed immigrants as a burden on the US, 44 per cent of those conservatives said yes, and only 13 per cent of Democrats did.

Another key consideration is that in certain immigrant communities a disproportionate number join the military. Therefore, they care about veterans' affairs. Donald Trump was very vocal on taking care of vets, particularly when it came to health care. Hillary Clinton was viewed here again as an extension of the Obama regime. There were scandals involving the Department of Veterans' Affairs on Obama's watch and massive increases in healthcare premiums, announced just two weeks before polling day – the average healthcare premium rose by 39 per cent, a significant increase no matter one's household income.

According to the Department of Defence, young people in Florida aged between eighteen and twenty-four are around twice as likely to join the armed forces as their counterparts across the country. The highest recruitment figures by state come from Florida, Georgia and Maine. North Dakota and Utah are among the lowest.

Of course, let's not forget that Donald Trump spent a good chunk of his time living in Florida, at his private club in West Palm Beach, Mar-a-Lago. Florida is famous for its 'snow bird' phenomenon – like Nancy and Jack, a couple who come from Ohio to Florida every winter.

Nancy is one of the most curious women I've ever met. She's eighty years young, her husband Jack is eighty-two and she is white, Christian and very house-proud.

She and her husband live in her family home and every winter, from November to March or thereabouts, they pack up their camper van and head off on the fifteen-hour drive to Florida. They break the journey with overnight stays in various places along the way.

When they get to Florida they stay in a trailer that they share at various times throughout the summer with six other families. But Nancy says she doesn't know how much longer they'll be able to do that, given their age. Nancy also has pulmonary fibrosis and isn't very sure of her future. This might be her last winter in Florida, she confides.

Their house is on a corner lot. Back when she was a child, that lot was formed because it was on a bend in the main road and her father had a petrol pump there. But after a few serious crashes on the corner, the pump was eventually taken out for safety. Now they've a pristine home, with a white-painted deck complete with swinging porch seat. Out back is a shed, also spick and span. It's adorned with a very large Trump flag – which Nancy tells me her daughter bought for them in the local discount store – and a homemade banner of support. It's a plank of wood that has been painted white and the words 'Just Trump It' stencilled on. Below that is what looks to be a hand-carved wooden cut-out of the star-spangled banner itself.

Nancy and Jack are very religious. Their political beliefs are determined by their religious beliefs – nothing new there. But they are very stringent in what they think. They are vehemently pro-life. Jack describes them as 'church-going people', but that gives the impression they go to mass every Sunday like big swathes of the population and pick and choose in the meantime. No. 'I'm good in regard to what the Bible says. We uphold God's word and that's important in this country because of so many things that are going on right now.' He stops and sighs. 'There's a disrespect for God and country. These people that promote all this ... *stuff* ... I call it *stuff*, which is what it amounts to in the end. We're just concerned about young children growing up, or even being born. Yet to be born. We're concerned about that and about how God feels about it.'

Nancy was afraid that if Hillary Clinton had been elected she would have put 'liberal judges' on the Supreme Court bench. That, she said, would have meant the US was headed 'down the drain'. She shakes her head and gets as agitated as a genteel older lady can when she says she can't believe that Christians would for vote for 'people like her, that believes in gay rights, abortion and everything that's sinful, when God calls it "abomination"'.

Nancy moved into the house she lives in now when she was twelve years old. Her husband, Jack, is from the next state over, Kentucky, but he moved to Ohio when he was in the eighth grade, aged about twelve or thirteen. They met when they were in junior high school and he says the first thing she did was laugh at him.

She denies that but it's clear they have a strong bond after almost seventy years together.

But when it comes to her country, she's worried and upset.

'We've gone away from Christian values in the last eight years, and it's just unbelievable.' (The unspoken words here being the *Barack Obama* years.)

'We have twelve great-grandchildren, going to have another one, and I just, I don't know what's going to happen to them. If you grow up without God in our country anymore and you let everybody in, that you don't know what they are, how we going to afford it?'

So concerned is she about the fate of America that she includes the USA in her prayers every night. So do many of her summer friends in Florida and her winter friends in Ohio.

'Oh, I pray for it every night. Every night. I pray for it. But we've gone so far. I look back and I wonder if God is going to bless our country. There've been so many people that's not thankful for what we've got. We've had good values in our country for a lot of years but it's gone down the last eight. So, I don't know. The good have to suffer with the bad. And I couldn't hardly blame God if he turns his back on us because it's bad.'

To be clear, Nancy would consider the election of Hillary Clinton as an example of God 'turning his back' on the United States.

Furthermore, no part of her felt any sort of pang of empathy, of feminist drive, to vote for the first female president of the United States. Turnout among women voters was only one percentage point higher in 2016 than it was in 2012 – a little higher than in the past, presumably because some, but clearly not enough, were motivated by the chance of seeing a female president. But not Nancy.

'No, women shouldn't be in. There's a place for women and it's not the head of our country. I don't care whether it's her or

whatever woman. No, definitely not. No. I don't care who they'd
run.'

In my lifetime, I've never heard another woman verbalise that
there is any job on this earth that a woman couldn't do. They may
issue a qualification to that statement, such as a woman can do any
job she wants, as long as she's doing it as well as men do and isn't
just there for the sake of gender balance.

So it floored me when, in the cool stillness of an Autumn sunset
one evening, a woman twice my age told me there is one job she
thinks a woman has no right doing: being the president. It further
floored me because I come from a country where there have been
two female presidents. Was she implying *they* were not as good as
men would have been?

Nancy explained further why she didn't want a woman, any
woman, in the Oval Office.

'Because ... I don't know ... women ... eh ... I don't know how
to put it.' She paused, looked down for a beat and then looked
up again. 'It's a place for men. Women are supposed to be in the
home and taking care of their families and their husbands. You
know what I mean ... No, it's no place for women. Of course a lot
of women are in the Congress and the Senate and all of that, but
not the head of our country. That's a big job. You can't take care of
your home, and be at home and be out all over the world.'

If she views women in such a precise and protected way, what
about how Donald Trump talks about women?

'I'm like most people. I really don't like a lot of words that
Donald uses, but we can't look at that.'

Her husband agrees: 'we have a man that is crude, but he's not
corrupt. That is the big difference. His vocabulary, he's rough. He's
not politically correct, as we've been accustomed to for all these
years. He's different.'

Jack is attracted to Donald Trump's vision to 'Make America
Great Again'. That's what he really likes about him. 'We've slipped

fifty years back in this country in the last five. I think America would be great again if we could go back even just five years.'

He has a particular problem with the views young people have now and what they are being taught in school. 'Some of them hardly remember 9/11. They don't know about the Cold War, about the Berlin Wall falling. They're not being taught history. Donald Trump has pledged to do away with the US Department of Education and hand it back to the states.' President Trump has promised to end what's referred to as 'common core' education – a regularised, universal, standardised syllabus that all school children in the United States must study. It is controversial in conservative areas because they would prefer to teach certain subjects, such as religious education, civics and history, from a different perspective. Jack wants that. Teachers, he said, 'could then once more teach a course of writing, instead of printing and looking at a computer all day'.

'I vote Republican, because I believe in Republican principles,' he says.

So how does Nancy square her Christian beliefs with her support for Donald Trump – a twice-divorced man who has children with three different wives and cheated on one wife with her eventual successor? A man who has left a trail of business partners, customers and clients filing lawsuits against him? A man who, until the election, was ambivalent about abortion but then said during an interview on the campaign trail that women who had abortions should be held criminally liable?

Nancy explains. 'Well, he's got a lot of people behind him. He's got a lot of smart people that's backing him and I think they can be a big help to him. But I think he's gotten older now and maybe more, what do you say? Maybe watches more what he'll say. But he's raised good children, you've got to look at that. Very good children.'

But then she puts it in even more stark terms for me. 'If you don't have Christian values, you're doomed.'

Many people like Nancy and Jack actually up sticks and live in Florida year round once they hit a certain age. The county with the largest number of older people in the US is here in Florida – Sumter County. The median age of its population is 62.7 years old. The median age for the whole country is 37.8 years. Sumter County voted for Donald Trump in large numbers – his margin of victory there was 29 percentage points.

Four counties that, like Sumter, are largely white and have an older age population gave Donald Trump huge numbers of votes, which helped to eat into the lead that Hillary Clinton had built up coming out of the densely populated and majority Democratic Miami-Dade region. According to the Census Bureau, 3.3 million Americans are aged over fifty, no longer in the workforce and have moved states for their retirement. These people are overwhelmingly clustered in Florida, in Arizona and along the coast of South Carolina. They are statistically more likely to hold conservative views and be wealthy. All the more reason to be naturally attracted to Donald Trump.

Massachusetts

NOT ALL IRISH AMERICANS ARE CLINTON-LOVING DEMOCRATS

There's a meeting once a month in mid-western Massachusetts, deep in Democratic country. The club is full of older gentlemen who do good works, a sort of Rotary Club-type organisation. Many of those here worked for that great Irish-American Massachusetts dynasty – Kennedy World. Some for JFK, others for his brothers Robert and Ted. The expression 'dyed in the wool Democrats' could have been invented for these men. They are hard-working, lower middle class and they value unions and pay packets and fairness. Most of them could trace their heritage back to Ireland. Some would have to go back six or seven generations; for others it's their grandparents or even a parent.

At a meeting in this community hall in late September, in that wonderful time of year that is a New England fall, several of them turned up wearing red baseball caps with the familiar Make America Great Again slogan. They were not asked to remove them. That was only partly due to the right of freedom of expression guaranteed by the first amendment to the constitution; it was also because, it seemed anyway, most of those in the room were Donald Trump supporters.

Massachusetts was never going to vote as a state for Donald Trump – that would really have been quite the turnaround, and actually Hillary Clinton won by a bigger margin here in 2016 than Barack Obama did in 2012. However, what is remarkable is that pockets of this blue state did like the message that Trump was selling. A great number of Irish Americans liked what he was selling.

Take Wilbraham, Massachusetts for example. It's a suburb of the reasonably sized city of Springfield. It is steeped in Irish heritage. There's an Irish night in the library every year and 11.8 per cent of the population claims Irish heritage. However, it is one of the counties in this state where Donald Trump got far more votes than Hillary Clinton. It has green fields and rolling hills, not dissimilar to Ireland. It makes sense that all those years ago Irish emigrants would have got this far and settled, in a new country, far from home, but with visual reminders of the Emerald Isle. The town was originally almost entirely comprised of farms, but as populations rose, in the wake of the Second World War, the farmland was gradually replaced with housing developments. Textile manufacturing was originally the main industry, and the Collins paper mill was the largest employer. The town was well served by roads and the Scantic and Chicopee rivers.

Some of those in Wilbraham who voted for Trump were from immigrant families themselves. Irish Americans whose ancestors had lived through periods of 'No Irish Need Apply' signage were attracted to a candidate who was actively encouraging a 'No Mexicans Need Apply' or a 'No Muslims Need Apply' policy towards newer immigrants.

Louis Murray is a proud Irish American. He lives in Boston and is a financial planner. But he's also a proud Republican and staunch Donald Trump fan. He became a part of the Trump movement pretty early on, he says.

Around 10 per cent of the American population claim Irish heritage, but the highest percentage of Irish blood found in the most populous metro areas in the United States is in Boston. There one in five people claim Irish ancestry.

Lou Murray grew up living with his Irish grandparents, his grandfather from Kerry and his grandmother from Cork. He's very close to his cousins in Munster and regularly travels over for visits. Two of his brothers lived and worked in Dublin and Limerick for a time.

As a financial planner of Irish American descent in Boston, he has lots of Irish-born clients and says he regularly discusses Donald Trump with them.

'I'm a 100 per cent Trump man. What is it about him that makes me excited? I guess, in a word, it would be sovereignty. The same reasons that my grandparents left Ireland at the time of the civil war – Donald Trump wants to make sure that America has security. A secure border, a secure economy and people are secure in their homes and in their persons. I'm from Boston and we experienced a horrible act of evil, some people would call it tragedy, but the right word is evil, and that was the Boston marathon bombing. And the people of Ireland were so good, they poured their hearts out to us. We lost a little boy in the neighbourhood right across the bridge from me.'

He's talking about eight-year-old Martin Richard, one of the three people killed when two homemade bombs exploded near the finish line of the Boston marathon on Patriots' Day, 15 April 2013. Over 260 people were injured. The now infamous Tsarnaev brothers were responsible for that bombing. During the manhunt that followed the bombing, the brothers killed a fourth person, an MIT police officer.

Dzhokhar is currently in prison, convicted and sentenced to death; he is appealing that decision. His older brother Tamerlan was killed during a police shootout in Watertown following that manhunt in the greater Boston area. Trying to make his getaway in a stolen vehicle that night, Dzhokhar also drove over his brother. The brothers had become US citizens but were born in Chechnya. By the time of the bombings, their parents had left the US and were living in the Russian republic of Dagestan. Dzhokhar's lengthy trial in Boston heard that first Tamerlan and then Dzhokhar had been radicalised through Internet materials. They had even learned online how to make the pressure-cooker nail bombs they'd carried in backpacks that fateful day.

Although Lou himself is the grandson of Irish immigrants, he is very clear that in his opinion the current US immigration policy is what led to the situation where these two young men could wreak such chaos. During the trial they were described as 'home grown terrorists' who had come to hate the United States.

'That was because we just let any old person into the country, and we have to be more careful of who we're taking in, where they're coming from and what are their real intentions. Do they want to become Americans? The Irish who've come to America have embraced American culture. We have, I guess I would call it, a new breed of immigrant that's invading Europe and invading America, and they don't want to become American.'

He is referring to immigrants who practise the Muslim faith. It is a sweeping generalisation, and the use of the word 'invading' is clearly deliberate on Lou's part. This is the same group singled out by then candidate Donald Trump on the campaign trail as people whose entry he would institute a ban to prohibit. Of all refugees who entered the US in 2016, 46 per cent of them were Muslims – 38,901 – but they were refugees, not immigrants moving for economic or other reasons. In 2016, most of the refugees admitted to the US came from the Democratic Republic of the Congo, followed by Syria, Burma, Iraq and Somalia.

Just like Donald Trump, Lou Murray has very strong feelings about migrants coming from the Middle East. 'They want to wear their niqabs and hijabs and they want to adopt Sharia and we've had a bombing in Boston, we've had a bombing in Orlando, we've had San Bernardino. We've had Nice, we've had Paris, we've had Belgium. The western world has gotta wake up – in America we're waking up and we're embracing Donald Trump.'

Lou distinguishes between different types of immigrants. Living and growing up in Boston, he says he has 'a lot' of friends who are 'undocumented Irish' and are supporting Donald Trump 'because they don't know about their security when they're walking down the street in Boston'. He also believes that, although Donald Trump has made very direct comments about stamping out illegal immigration and deporting those in the US without papers, he doesn't mean to do that to the Irish.

'Donald Trump is a fan of Ireland. He has a beautiful property in Ireland which is one of his treasures. He is going to work for the Irish to help get them legalised. I think I could say that he would try to work with the Western Europeans who are in the United States who are working and paying taxes, that they don't have anything to fear from a Donald Trump presidency.'

Just the opposite, in fact, argues Lou. 'They have everything to cheer about because look what's happened. We've had eight years of President Obama. He had two years where he had a full House and a full Senate. He didn't do anything for the Irish. He could have legalised all the Irish that were here.'

His point is valid. Barack Obama did have a 'sweet spot' of two years when Democrats held all three 'houses' – the House of Representatives, the Senate and the White House. That was the best chance of getting immigration reform passed. The prospect diminished from mid-2014 onwards to today, where almost no-one holds any realistic hope that a path to legalisation will be offered for those here without the correct paperwork – not any time soon, anyway.

It's not just immigration, though. Lou Murray is a Trump supporter for the same reasons as many of those right up through the Appalachian region that ultimately helped him to be declared president: the economy, job creation, making things financially better for him and his fellow Americans. Lou likes the insular, protectionist policy defined by 'America First'.

'Donald Trump is focused on getting rid of these one-sided trade deals. Think about the Irish – they came to Lowell, they came to Boston, they came to Worcester, they came to all these great factory towns, all those factories we've lost through trade agreements that were one sided. We have these massive, massive trade deficits – everything's made in China or in other countries. They're reaping all the benefits of our spending and our hard work and there's no reason why we can't, because of technology, make a lot of these things right here, right back in America again, and put our own people to work and buy our own goods.'

Lou says his motivation here is just like the motivation of those who voted for Brexit: a desire to be self-sufficient and self-reliant. In truth, though, except for those who actively take a keen interest in British, Irish or European affairs, very few people in the US are interested in Brexit. What happened in Britain was rarely, if ever, cited as a reason for voting a certain way.

From very early in the primary season, Lou Murray had faith in Donald Trump. Even in a traditional Democratic stronghold like Massachusetts, he campaigned loudly and frequently for the businessman. He even used his 2016 annual leave to go the Republican National Convention as a delegate.

'I took my summer vacation to come here and support him and to be part of this event and to further the American process. I would much rather have gone to see my cousins in Kerry and Cork and played a little golf myself and climbed in the national park and had a swim at Inch Beach and things like that. But I'm here because I believe he's going to win. I believe he's going to shock the political establishment and he has done it all the way.'

'Trump is for real. He's a different sort of politician. He's a populist and he's a nationalist, and as you can see with the Brexit campaign, that is what's very popular right now, all over the world. It's the year of the outsider and he's the outsider.'

Lou describes Trump's blitzing through the primary season as 'dragon-slaying', and while he thinks Trump appeals to people because he is 'future-orientated and positive looking', he thinks part of his success nationally is due to how poor a prospect Hillary Clinton is.

'She's old news. We went through Clinton-gate, file-gate, travel-gate, email-gate. She's compromised our national security at a time when we're under attack from Islamic extremists. Why would we want to put someone into office who has compromised our national security? It doesn't make sense. It doesn't wash, ultimately, with the voting public.'

Lou sums up his thoughts on President Trump like this: 'I think Trump is a pretty conservative guy and I'm happy with him being our standard bearer for the Republican Party.'

President Trump likes to associate himself with the actions and legacy of the fortieth president of the United States, Ronald Reagan. Reagan considered himself Irish. His great-great-grandfather Michael O'Regan left County Tipperary during the Great Irish Famine of the 1840s – like so many others. Through the generations the O'Regan surname morphed into Reagan. The Reagan Foundation goes as far as to say the late president 'revered' his Irish ancestry. A joke told by the former Canadian prime minister Brian Mulroney about Ronald Reagan at his wife Nancy's funeral even finished with a punchline about how he was 'an Irish guy who had married up'.

He attracted many Democrats to vote for him. So many they were given their own moniker of 'Reagan Democrats'. Trump too seems to have attracted some of the traditional Democratic supporters into his camp, though not as many as Reagan and not enough to be described as a cohort.

———

Although heavily unionised, members of the law-enforcement community provided plenty of support for Donald Trump – perhaps not in New York City, but in Boston and further afield – men and women in uniform who regularly stumped for Trump on the campaign trail and carried that support for him through into his presidency. Milwaukee sheriff David Clarke was one of Trump's biggest law-enforcement cheerleaders – he even addressed the Republican National Convention in July 2016 on his behalf. So loyal was Sheriff Clarke that his name was briefly in the mix to become FBI director once President Trump had fired James Comey.

One Irish American sheriff who can't speak highly enough of President Trump is Carolyn Welsh, better known as Sheriff Bunny. She's been sheriff of Chester County, a suburb of Philadelphia in Pennsylvania, for nearly twenty years. Like Boston, Philadelphia is another centre for Irish immigration. Sheriff Bunny runs Annie Oakley Gun Safety classes for women in her district and is also a proud grandmother – on the day we first speak she is brimming with pride at the success of two of her grandchildren in the World Irish Dancing Championships in Dublin. Her nine-year-old grandson came first in his category, she proudly announces. Her nine-year-old granddaughter came third, and they finished first in the 'two-hander' category for their age. She says she's not entirely sure of the origin of her Irish blood, and has never fully traced it, but that it's on her father's side. Her mother's side is Scottish.

Her Trump credentials are beyond question. She rallied up and down Pennsylvania – the state that officially put him over the top at the Republican Convention – for him. A petite blonde who radiates sassiness, she's been known to wear a sequin-bedazzled Trump T-shirt with the American flag fashioned into the shape of a stiletto with the words 'Trump Girl' alongside it. When sheriffs from across America were invited to the White House during Trump's first weeks in office so the new president could thank them for their support, she was not only on the invite list: she was seated right beside him. When the president hosted a rally in Harrisburg, Pennsylvania to mark his first hundred days in office, it was Sheriff Bunny who warmed up the several-thousand-strong crowd before he came on stage.

'Oh, I'm Trump all the way,' she says. 'I was a very early supporter because my feeling was that he, above all others, brought a different perspective to the presidency, being not the usual establishment candidate, not beholden to special interests. Not a Washington "insider" and not the usual politician. I found his message to be very populist, very refreshing and very focused on his theme, which is making America great again, that he really cared about the people and putting America first. To me that was refreshing because I think politicians on both sides, and I'm a Republican but I will criticise them as much as I will the Democrats, many of them have been there a long time. I fear sometimes their decisions are more focused on winning the next election instead of what's best for the people.'

She says first and foremost she was attracted to Donald Trump's messages as an individual, but wearing her sheriff's hat, he was the best option for the law enforcement community. 'He has a very strong law and order message. His message was that he supports local, state and federal police. In other words, he was endorsed by the Federal Border Patrol, which was very unusual. His position on supporting federal agencies, state agencies and municipal and township, whether they're police or county sheriffs, was that he was a very strong supporter. He really has great respect for law enforcement.'

That 'respect' for law enforcement has been missing of late, she says.

Although she is a card-carrying Republican, on the issue of law enforcement she plays straight down the line. She's been a sheriff since the year 2000 so has been there through two Republican presidential terms (George W. Bush) and two Democratic ones (Barack Obama). In recent years, the behaviour of local sheriff's department personnel and police officers in urban areas has been brought into sharp focus with the officer-related shootings that have been captured on social media. The highest-profile cases that have resulted in protest marches have been race-related. In some instances, charges have been brought against officers, and in some cases, controversially, they have not.

Sheriff Bunny says the handling of those cases by the Department of Justice and wider administration under Barack Obama was not well received by many working in law enforcement.

'They were too quick to judge in many cases, with cases that were made public. And before facts were even out they were too quick to judge the law-enforcement officer. I'm not saying that there aren't law-enforcement officers that aren't all perfect, and there are certainly some bad apples. I'm not saying that. But before facts were out, often the law-enforcement officer was the one made ... was the one criticised or ... well, criticised is the word I'll use. So with someone criticised first in circumstances before the facts were even out, that's very, very bad for the morale of law enforcement. It's very, very bad for men and women. My guys every day put on a bulletproof vest and a badge and a gun, and they go out to protect and serve, and they need to know that somebody has their back. And for many years, from the top down, I think the feeling was that law enforcement was not supported.'

She's referring to the comments made by Barack Obama and his two attorney generals, Eric Holder and Loretta Lynch, following some of those officer-involved shootings. There was commentary, but then there was the establishment of community policing bodies and a review of relationships. Another police chief I spoke to in Maryland said the prospect of an officer-involved shooting involving a white officer and a black victim was what kept him up at night – that no matter the circumstances, or who was right and who was wrong, there was an assumption forming that the officer would be considered racist.

That commentary 'from the top' has resulted in a diminution of respect for police and law-enforcement personnel, says Bunny. 'I think the general lack of respect for law enforcement was prevalent – the idea that you could taunt or aggravate a law-enforcement officer, the general disregard for authority. But I see that in lots of places, sometimes even in schools now, unfortunately.' Bunny says she's seen what she describes as a 'disregard for authority and a disrespect for law enforcement'. There is a reason why citizens are feeling that way, she quickly adds: there was a feeling that law enforcement personnel had a certain immunity from prosecution for unlawful shootings. That there was an 'us against them' culture, and police officers didn't relate to or understand the citizens they were policing. So, in turn, citizens have lost respect for the police and taunt them, but officers are at times afraid to respond lest they be deemed aggressive or racist. She says she's seen a real 'degrading' of the relationship. 'It really does affect the morale of men and women who are on the street.'

Donald Trump provides a safety net for Sheriff Bunny and her officers and the sheriffs across the country. The Fraternal Order of Police, the largest police union in the US, which has over 330,000 law-enforcement members, endorsed Donald Trump ahead of the election, even though it caused much internal debate, particularly among African American officers. One of the industry magazines, *Police Magazine*, surveyed its subscribers ahead of the election and found that 84 per cent of law-enforcement officers intended supporting Mr Trump.

Sheriff Bunny is not surprised.

'He has our back and of course we have his. It's good to hear from the top that he will put people in place that have respect, not only for law enforcement but for the military and for the citizens. He believes in the citizens first. He puts America first. That has been his position all through the campaign and it's his position now as commander-in-chief.'

Chester County is one of the three original Pennsylvania counties established by William Penn in 1682. It's the wealthiest county in Pennsylvania and one of the top twenty-five wealthiest counties in the US.

The sheriff describes it as 'a safe county'. Just about half a million people live there. 'We have some pockets of challenging places with some higher crime than others but we have a good county,' she says. 'We don't have the challenges that Philadelphia has, but so far I'm very pleased. And we look forward to much greater support from Washington.'

As a sheriff and supporter of the second-amendment right to bear arms, she was also impressed by Trump's position on firearms.

'I think he's a great supporter of the second amendment. I think he's a great supporter of the constitution. So I think all of those things are pieces of what his campaign was about and it certainly is what his presidency is about.'

———

In my experience, Irish Americans mostly tend to be Catholic, and tend to be more devoted Catholics than perhaps the modern Irish population as a whole. For example, I've met far more people in the US who observe meat-free Fridays, adhere strictly to Lent and attend mass regularly than I know in Ireland. Many Irish-American events still begin with some sort of prayer or blessing. I've also met a reasonable number of young Irish Americans who will not move in with a romantic partner unless there has been a marriage proposal. That decision is not to appease their traditional parents, as it perhaps might be in Ireland, but is to meet their own exacting standards. These are obviously anecdotal observations – no survey exists to chart it.

But it is these strict Irish Catholic viewpoints that drew some Irish American Democrats to Donald Trump. In election 2016, as in every US election, the issue of abortion came front and centre. Where a candidate stands on abortion will make them attractive or seal their fate in the eyes of voters.

Much furore was caused with Donald Trump's candidacy, as it initially appeared that he had an equivocal position on abortion. He was pitched alongside Hillary Clinton, who had the traditional Democratic liberal viewpoint of a woman's right to choose. Quickly Republican leadership whispered in his ear, metaphorically speaking, that his position would have to change and he would have to become staunchly pro-life. For some people, turned off by both candidates, this became the deciding factor.

Democrats are viewed as the 'abortion party', and while this attracts many voters to them, it turns many off.

Thomas Groome is a professor of theology and religious education at Boston College. Originally from County Kildare, and a former Catholic priest, he's been living in the US for almost half a century. He says when he moved to the US originally, he was advised by a cousin that Irish Catholics voted for Democrats. He has argued on the pages of the *New York Times* that the Democratic Party needs to soften its stance on abortion if it is to attract Catholics back. He was also an adviser to the Hillary Clinton campaign, contributed to many speeches she made on abortion and other religious issues and wrote a position paper ahead of the presidential debates on abortion, counselling her to take a more nuanced position. He's now involved in advising the Democratic party ahead of the 2018 midterm elections, and is giving them the same advice: develop a 'nuanced' position on the landmark abortion case of *Roe v Wade*.

In that judgement, handed down in 1973, the US Supreme Court ruled that a state law (in Texas) banning abortion except to save the life of the mother was unconstitutional. The court ordered that individual states were forbidden from banning or regulating any aspect of abortion during the first trimester of pregnancy, but that they could enact regulations for the second and third trimesters. The court said states could enact laws protecting the life of the foetus/unborn child only in the third trimester but still had to include a provision to make an exception in order to protect the life of the mother.

The case of 'Jane Roe' originally came about because that pregnant woman could not afford to travel across state lines to have an abortion and said her constitutional rights were being breached as she had a right to terminate her pregnancy in a safe medical environment in the state where she lived.

Thomas Groome's opining promoted scores of letters to the editor of the *New York Times*, many of them from Irish American Catholics agreeing with him. They had found it very difficult to vote for Hillary Clinton, even as Democrats themselves, because of her view on abortion – that reproductive rights were the purview of the woman involved and that states had no role in regulating them. She vowed to defend the Roe v. Wade judgement; Trump vowed to campaign to have it overturned and return decision-making to the individual states, as it had been before.

As James Phelan from New Jersey put it: 'I'm an Irish Italian Catholic who would normally vote Democratic, but the incessant and strident pro-abortion stance of the Democratic Party sickens me and perhaps many others in the country.'[10]

Or Gabriel Moran from New York: 'Hillary Clinton's loss of the Catholic vote was tragic and unnecessary. Many Catholics were put off by the tone and emphasis of Mrs Clinton's answer to the loaded question of "partial birth" abortion in the third presidential debate. She could have affirmed everything that she did while acknowledging a context of moral sensitivity.'

That attitude plays out in the voting records from 2016. Hillary Clinton lost the white Catholic vote by 23 percentage points – a massive margin. Overall, Catholics make up about one-quarter of the available electorate, a sizeable voting bloc. The cities with the highest percentages of Catholic voters are Boston, New York, Chicago, Los Angeles and San Diego – all cities with high percentages of immigrants. Given the statistics, we can deduce that a good portion of those voting 'white Catholics' were Irish Americans. She lost the overall Catholic vote by seven percentage points. In those states where the election was extremely close – Wisconsin, Michigan, Pennsylvania – she lost by such a narrow margin that every factor has to be looked at. For all the voters that sided with Trump because of his tough-talking position on jobs and economic renewal, did others side with him because he was pro-life?

Thomas Groome is convinced many did. He argues that by blindly offering unconditional support for the Roe v Wade decision, Mrs Clinton left herself 'no wriggle room'. He argues that it is the 'defining issue' in many swing states, and that there are strong pockets of Catholics in Pennsylvania and Florida that were turned off by her stringent position – states that Obama, with a more nuanced position, won, and states that Clinton lost.

Thomas was originally educated in Ireland and ordained in Carlow Cathedral in 1968 before going to minister in Dodge City, Kansas, alongside one of his brothers. He has lived in the US ever since and left the priesthood after seventeen years, later marrying and having a son. He says that Irish Americans, and American Catholics in general, consider their faith to be 'a very serious issue', more so than Catholics in Ireland do. He says that Catholics in the US tend to be 'better informed and grounded in their faith'. He explains that because they've chosen Catholicism in a country where it is not the majority religion, they have attended extra-curricular study classes and so are often more connected to and informed by the key tenets of the religion, more than many Irish people, who are – traditionally anyway – Catholic almost 'by default'.

The US Conference of Catholic Bishops issued a directive in advance of the election, offering guidance on how people should vote. In 'Forming Consciences for Faithful Citizenship', agreed following a meeting of all US bishops in November 2015, the bishops didn't make a formal pronouncement to their faithful. They urged thorough consideration of the candidates and declined from endorsing one or the other. However, they did permit the faithful to 'legitimately disqualify a candidate from receiving support' if 'a candidate's position on a single issue promotes an intrinsically evil act, such as legal abortion'.[11]

While many Irish people in Ireland may identify with the Democratic Party, as does much of Western Europe, the Irish American community is no longer quite so black and white, or rather red and blue. Apart from the Catholic belief system, the Republican Party also stands for low taxes, personal responsibility and individual liberty, and a smaller, less intrusive role for the federal government – all viewpoints that perhaps resonate with those of Irish heritage or who grew up in homes listening to tales of the civil war and Irish republicanism. In addition, the Irish in America have long had a strong sense of civic duty and public service. That is demonstrated in the twenty-two US presidents who claim Irish ancestry (there are no indications of Irish blood in President Trump yet, but his mother was Scottish so there is Celtic blood) and the myriad of Irish surnames in successive congressional rolls on Capitol Hill. In America, Irish ethnicity is not solely the preserve of either party. More Medal of Honour winners have claimed Irish heritage than any other ethnic grouping. The Irish American Democrats, particularly on the east coast, are far more organised, and therefore far more vocal, than the Irish American Republicans are, but that is not to say they are not a solid presence. The Irish American Republicans grouping was incorporated in 1868. The group currently known as the Irish American Democrats was founded in 1996, but various organisations existed in different formats before that.

Election-planning and vote-management officials in both the Republican National Committee and the Democratic National Committee agree that there is no 'Irish vote' anymore. Of course there once was. In the mid-nineteenth century, when large numbers of Irish arrived to concentrated areas on the east coast, and in particular were courted in Boston and New York, there was a voting bloc. But now the vote is split. Irish Americans vote based on their other value systems, not the fact that they're Irish. They vote as Americans, whether they favour abortion or taxes or same-sex marriage or trade or economic policy. They've assimilated – that is what happens with immigrant populations over time. The policies that defined the Irish in Ireland dissolved in the great melting pot of US culture. The literature, the music, the dance and some of the cooking was preserved, but the outlook on life and political views were impacted by their environment. Donald Trump won 60 per cent of the white Catholic vote, and many of those are Irish Americans.

Ohio

PREACHER'S WIFE POPS PAIN PILLS IN PRISON

'Drugs are killing so many people in Ohio that cold-storage trailers are being used as morgues,' screamed the headline.[12] Bodies stored in refrigerated trucks over a weekend. Not at the scene of a large-scale natural disaster. But in Ohio. In America, the ninth wealthiest country in the world. The land of hope and glory. But not so hopeful and glorious if you're a crime-scene investigator in the Stark County coroner's office who has to request a cold-storage container to act as an overflow morgue for the weekend because by 3 p.m. on a Friday the bricks-and-mortar morgue is already full.

Ohio is experiencing a drug epidemic. So is much of so-called middle America. You don't hear a lot about it because none of these towns and cities are high on the tourist radar. No popular TV shows are set in these counties, and the US and international media have been so focused on the reality-TV show that was the 2016 presidential election campaign and the subsequent Trump White House that few resources are expended highlighting these areas.

The local authorities do what they can. Famously, in 2016 the East Liverpool police force, in Ohio, posted photographs on Facebook of two adults, overdosed on heroin, unconscious in a car, with a four-year-old boy sitting in the backseat.[13]

The police report makes for harrowing reading. At ten past three on a Wednesday afternoon in September, an off-duty police officer was driving in his own car when he noticed the car in front was 'driving very erratic weaving back and forth in the lane'. Up ahead, children were getting off a school bus, so the car braked hard and skidded to a stop. When the bus pulled away, the car stayed in the middle of the road before 'drifting ... in an angle and stopping'.

The off-duty police officer got out of his car and found a fifty-year-old woman unconscious and turning blue in the passenger seat. The forty-seven-year-old man driving the car just managed to say he was trying to take her to the hospital before he passed out too as he reached to restart the engine.

All the while, the woman's four-year-old son was sitting in a car-seat behind her. In the photographs he's wearing a brightly coloured dinosaur T-shirt; he looks confused and afraid.

The city authorities explained they had posted the images because they felt it was necessary to show the other side 'of this horrible drug' and to 'be a voice for the children caught up in this horrible mess'. They said they were 'well aware' that some would be offended by the shocking images, but they felt it was 'time that the non-drug using public' saw what the authorities were dealing with 'on a daily basis'. They said they hoped the story of this one little boy could 'convince another user to think twice about injecting this poison while having a child in their custody'. They added that they were willing to fight the problem 'until it's gone', and if that meant offending 'a few people along the way', they were prepared to pay that price.

Ultimately, in that case the drug addicts regained consciousness and the boy was taken by social services. That is deemed a successful outcome by Ohio standards. Lives damaged, but no lives lost.

The most recent figures from the Ohio Department of Health show 3,050 opioid-related deaths in 2015: the highest ever on record, a 775 per cent increase in twelve years. It's the fourth highest rate in the US. West Virginia has the highest rate of drug-related deaths, followed by New Hampshire, Kentucky, then Ohio, with the top five rounded out by Rhode Island.

In Ireland drug-related deaths account for 71 deaths per million. That's three times the European average, according to the latest figures from the European Monitoring Centre for Drugs and Drug Addiction. Here in Ohio, the rate is four times the Irish rate, with drug-related deaths accounting for about 277 out of every million.

Angie Pelphrey, a former drug addict who now runs the New Beginnings rehab centre, describes it as more than an epidemic. 'It's a tsunami, like a hurricane.' She says that sometimes two or three people a week pass away from drug overdoses in Pike County where she lives. There have been a few days where the local hospital has dealt with twenty overdoses in a day. 'It's very, very bad here.'

'A lot of people say it's due to being in a small town with not a lot to do,' she says. Many of the residents at her fifty-person treatment facility say they first tried drugs or alcohol somewhere between the ages of eight and ten.

Driving through this part of Ohio, it's idyllic. Nothing resembles a grotty heroin den, no graffiti and broken bottles that might be evident in a city. It's all green trees, open fields, picket fences, water towers and memorials to war veterans.

Turn a corner in the road and veer off onto a small country lane and you'll soon reach Angie's rehab centre. Pulling in from the road, you immediately see a big barbecue smoking drum. The large wooden deck of the main building is filled with young people playing some sort of card game. Two dogs run around the front yard, greeting approaching vehicles with the unbridled excitement and curiosity that all dogs do. A smaller outhouse-type building houses an office, and a larger building is set off to another side. It has big windows, with the curtains drawn against the heat. That's the female residential quarters and main classroom facility.

Following the news and police reports here, it's all about the heroin epidemic. But an arguably far nastier drug of choice is circulating too. Nastier because it is legal, acceptable and prescribed at will by medical professionals – pain pills, aka OxyContin.

'Yeah, I'm the preacher's wife that got sent to prison as a lying, thieving junkie.'

Angie knows all about pain pills. A glamorous blonde woman in her mid-forties, she's wearing tight jeans and an off-the-shoulder sweater. She looks fit and healthy – a poster girl for the term 'yummy mummy', perhaps. But that's now. Fifteen years ago a different Angie would have greeted me – one, she tells me, that would have caused me to clutch my handbag tightly, lock the car doors and drive off in a hurry.

Back then she was a paediatric nurse, a mother of three and a pastor's wife. She had a back injury and was sent to the first 'pain pill' clinic, which had opened 25 miles south in Portsmouth, on the border with Kentucky.

She was initially prescribed Lortab – a painkilling medication combining acetaminophen (paracetamol) and hydrocodone – an opioid, a narcotic. She says by her second month she was already taking about 220 of these a month to try to get relief from her back pain.

Looking back, she says she was already an addict by then, but because she was a respectable, God-fearing mom, wife and nurse, she didn't think so. An addict to her was someone shooting up in an alley, not someone popping a few pills for her bad back to get her through the day at work. Plus they were being prescribed to her professionally.

But fast forward two or three years and things got worse. By then she was stealing pain medications from patients in the hospital.

In 2004 she was arrested, charged, convicted and sentenced to two years in prison in the Ohio Reformatory for Women in Marysville, about a hundred miles away. She could have avoided prison if she went into a rehab programme, but as a nurse married to a pastor they made too much money, so she didn't qualify for any benefits or get access to any public rehab systems. The private cost of rehab was about $30,000 a month and not something her health insurance would cover. So she went to prison and served ten months of her sentence.

As many before her have said, she feels prison changed her.

'I saw people differently. I saw myself, finally, as one of them, somebody else that was incarcerated that had an issue or whatever may have happened to them. Growing up sometimes in church, you become judgemental. I was able to actually take that mask off and see people with my heart instead of my eyes.'

She swore that a lack of money would not stop anyone else getting the help they needed to kick a drug addiction.

It was a huge scandal in her conservative church community. The pastor's wife, arrested for stealing drugs in a hospital to feed her addiction. 'It was very difficult' but they got through it, she says. A lot of people called her husband and told him that 'as pastor, you need to divorce her'. They'd been married for fifteen years at that time and her husband turned to scripture to convince others to allow her to return. He now speaks to the residents here about enabling addicts, because Angie says he was her enabler at the time.

She persuaded what she calls her 'church family' to band together to open their own rehab centre. They started with just a handful of people. Now, in this one community in Southwest Ohio, they have fifty places for addicts – thirty-two men and sixteen women.

People stay for nine to twelve months and once they're clean they 'graduate'. But they don't throw anyone out, so currently they have four people living there who are 'clean' but just don't have anywhere to go.

At the centre, they use the services of the local hospital to help wean the addicts off their drug of choice, but mostly it's a case of going 'cold turkey'. 'It's a tough process,' says Angie. They pray a lot and read scripture.

There's a mixed bag of guests at this facility. They take turns on kitchen duty, but today everyone's excited. One of the current patients was a chef in a top restaurant in Columbus – the capital of Ohio and the biggest city in this state, about 70 miles north of here. He's got the drum smoker going and four fat, juicy hams are being barbecued. Every now and then he bastes them with apple juice. He's removing the husks from corn cobs to put them in the smoking drum as well. Then there are several big homemade pies for dessert.

Today this Columbus chef and recovering junkie has even cooked up his own special barbecue sauce, with a secret ingredient, he jokes.

Another man tells me he was a big baseball agent, doing really well for himself. He had a lot of money, a beautiful wife and a 'real cute kid'. He rolled high, partied well and lived hard, he says. When booze didn't work for him, he hit cocaine; when the high from that was fading, he started on heroin. He said he was in some of the nicest suites in the poshest hotels in the US, shooting up with gear he bought in alleyways from 'wasters'. Inevitably it all came crumbling down. He's embarrassed to admit, he says, that he ripped off all his friends. He knew he was doing it, 'but honestly I really didn't care. The high was more important. I wanted to feed my addiction more than I wanted to feed my kid.' He hopes his (soon to be ex-) wife will eventually forgive him and maybe one day he'll get to see his son, but for now he's getting ready to face some 'serious embezzlement and fraud charges'. He doesn't want to share the details but encourages me to keep an eye on the news in about a year's time.

As the matron here, Angie has noticed a change in the issues her clients have. The drug problem used to be pain pills, prescribed to all sorts of people, but now it's heroin, she says. And worse still, the drug dealers are mixing the drugs with other substances to save money. One of her residents admitted to being a former dealer. He told her harrowing tales of drug cocktails that were actually killing people. He and his fellow dealers cut the drugs with whatever they had to hand that was cheap. He didn't care who died as long as he got paid.

Angie says the heroin problem is as bad as it is in this area because of the availability. People are travelling from Florida to Michigan along Route 23 and 'bringing it right into our town and selling it – it's so much cheaper around here'.

She doesn't think there's a way to stop the supply: they just have to stop the market. They need more prevention measures, more education, more treatment facilities.

Part of Donald Trump's reason for building his signature 'wall' along the Mexican border is to stop drugs from being trafficked into the US. The drugs in this middle corridor of America are coming in through the sea port in Florida – beyond the reach of any wall.

Nevertheless, Angie says anything that might help is welcome. 'That would be amazing, if it's possible.' She's circumspect about how likely it would be that a wall would stop drug traffickers: 'they'll figure out another way'. But they're desperate for help in this area, so they'll give anything a try.

It's a split community, she says, half registered as Democrats, half as Republicans. But Trump is taking a harder line about stopping drugs – he's at least talking about it, she says.

It's coming near dinner time so the residents break up from an anger-management role-playing session for a little down-time before eating.

In one communal room, names are written all over the walls. It's the 'death wall', says Angie.

One of their residents didn't do so well after he left. He tried hard, she said, but the power of the drug was too strong. (She describes, in her own case, on one particularly dark occasion, her husband gave her a choice between one more pill and ever seeing her three daughters again. She's embarrassed about which option she chose that night.)

Five years ago, that former client, Anthony, passed away. They wrote his name on the wall to remind themselves of the lifelong battle an addict faces to not 'fall off the wagon'. The next day, she said, some of the others had written more names on the wall too. She was initially cross because it was supposed to be a sort of memorial to that one special young man. But the others explained to her they 'wanted to put their own family up as well'. Angie says they stopped counting when they reached 3,000 names of local people. 'We're writing one to two names a week up there now. It was one wall – now it has become the whole room.'

———

It's not just drug overdoses that are claiming lives here. It's the crime wave too. In Piketon, Ohio, population 2,146, eight members of one family were killed in April 2016 in what police say is linked to a drug-gang war.

Seven adults and one teenage boy of the Rhoden family were found shot dead in four trailers on family land but nobody has yet been charged in connection with it. The Ohio attorney general says whoever killed them was familiar with the victims, their homes and the surrounding areas.

At one point, ninety detectives were assigned to the case, but the remaining family members have done multiple interviews with local media outlets complaining about the lack of progress in the case. They circulate brightly coloured posters in the Pike County area, appealing for information about their murdered relatives: forty-year-old Christopher Rhoden Sr, his former wife, thirty-seven-year-old Dana Manley Rhoden, and their three children, nineteen-year-old Hanna Rhoden, sixteen-year-old Chris Rhoden

Jr and twenty-year-old Clarence 'Frankie' Rhoden; Clarence's twenty-year-old fiancée Hannah Hazel Gilley; Christopher Rhoden's older brother, Kenneth, aged forty-four; and their thirty-eight-year-old cousin Gary Rhoden. A newborn, an infant and another young child were left physically unharmed in the attack.

Another cousin, Josh Rhoden, was arrested in early 2017 on drug-trafficking charges as part of what Ohio Attorney General Mike DeWine described as a separate 'ongoing drug investigation', involving authorities from three counties and the US 23 Pipeline Major Crimes Task Force.

The US 23 Pipeline is the cause of much of the problem, according to authorities here. It's not an actual pipeline but a notional one, such is the volume of drugs trafficked along the highway US Route 23. That road runs from the seaport city of Jacksonville, Florida all the way through middle America (Georgia, North Carolina, Kentucky, Ohio) and on to the northern tip of Michigan at Mackinaw City – next stop Canada. The route is also known as the Sunrise Side Coastal Highway, but nobody in central Ohio calls it that. It's exclusively the Pipeline.

Billy Spencer is the mayor of Piketon. The Rhoden family members were all killed just outside the village. He doesn't want to talk about it – the investigation is open and ongoing – but he admits there is a problem with drugs here.

'Of course, there's users in town, and there's people that distribute. Sell and distribute the drugs.'

His sheriff and the other authorities are targeting the pushers.

'If you take care of the sale and distributors, then the users, that tends to take care of itself. They'll go somewhere else or move. I guess ultimately that's the best solution. Move somewhere else.'

The village of Piketon is right on the edge of Route 23, the Pipeline, a big cause of their problems as Billy sees it.

'They come from Detroit down through Columbus and go south of here. We've had our issues with drugs, just like any other community, but we're very active here. We've had a lot of success in putting some criminals away and kept a lot of it out of town through some of our efforts, as far as at least a prescription drug problem.'

He says they're very active in pursuit of drug dealers but it remains a problem. But he is hopeful a new addition to the team will help.

'We're about a week away from getting our drug dog,' he tells me proudly. 'That'll help us a lot.'

When he came into office in 2003, he made a pledge to make Piketon drug free. He takes an 'aggressive' approach, he says, along with the sheriff's department and the police department.

But the mass murder on the edge of the village didn't help matters. The continued drug-trafficking charges don't either. In January 2017, three people overdosed in the town in the space of two and a half hours. (Remember, the total population is 2,146). One eighteen-year-old man died. The cause was a bad batch of heroin laced with Carfentanil, an elephant tranquiliser. The person charged with trafficking and supplying the drugs was a thirty-nine-year-old woman who had two children in her home while she was dealing drugs.

At that stage, the Piketon authorities 'declared war on drugs' in this area and went on a five-day major drugs bust. By the sixth week of 2017, they'd already exhausted their police overtime budget by $10,000, according to Pike County Sheriff Charles Reader. But it all comes down to money and resources. That level of expenditure is not sustainable for a small community like this, so success in their war on drugs will be difficult, if not impossible.

In this community, as in many others across America, 'junkies' are not young people living on park benches: they're middle-aged. They're parents of young children. They're housewives.

Of the drug deaths in Ohio last year, about a third were aged between twenty-five and thirty-four and more than half of the women who died from drugs were aged between thirty-five and sixty-five.

But despite the deathly shadows in the village, the people are like so many in this part of the country, in Appalachia. They are poorer and whiter, with lower levels of education than the rest of the country statistically, but their friendliness and welcoming spirits are disarming. They're not used to seeing visitors from another country and only want to put the best of the village on display.

The mayor explains: 'We're mostly just country people, to be honest with you. Hard-working, for the most part. Religious, for the most part. It's just a good place to live, to raise a family, to have a home. If you want the nightlife or something, you might have to go into Columbus, or something like that.'

————

At the New Beginnings rehab centre, where the recovering addicts are hovering around the smoker drum, the smell of the meat is intoxicating.

While Angie goes off to answer a phone, a school bus pulls up. Out jumps a very small girl, who looks like she could be ten or eleven years old, but she's actually seventeen. She says, in a matter of fact way, that she's probably so petite and childlike because of all the drugs she took from age thirteen up. But who knows?

She animatedly tells another worker what happened in school that day, with the same fervour and excitement that a small child might use to tell their mother about the day's travails. It seems this teenager, let's call her Anna, has a close girlfriend in school and that girlfriend has her own problems – she's a former addict too, but she now has difficulty controlling her temper. There are a lot of drugs in the local high school, she says, as an almost throwaway comment. Today there was an altercation with some other girls – who sound like your average straight-out-of-a-high-school-movie teen bullies. Whatever happened, Anna practised what Angie and the others had taught her about staying calm and walking away from conflict, but the other young woman lost her temper, lashed out and is now suspended.

Anna tells me she wants to join the military as soon as she finishes school. That's her dream. She already has the buzzcut and works out with weights as much as she can to build the physique required. Although she's hiding those muscles today behind men's khaki baggy clothing, a few sizes too big for her. Getting good grades in school is essential to the application process, as is not getting expelled. That happened once before during the height of her addiction and it can't happen again. She's resolute. She has dreams and ambitions now that were not part of her early childhood. At home, she never thought she could do or be anything, but now she knows she can.

Just then, in a quite dramatic way, a clearly vulnerable woman stumbles out of the dormitory building, squinting against the low evening sun. She's a new arrival to the facility. She's about my age, but her grey pallor, lank hair and hunched-over posture indicate that her life and mine couldn't be more different.

Angie tells me this woman just arrived about an hour before I did. Her father drove her. She's been on heroin for twenty years and he just can't take it anymore. He dumped her here with all of her belongings in black sacks. I count twenty of them. Her entire life, almost four decades, stuffed into bags. The stilettos of mismatched shoes pierce the plastic in places. Fur collars and bikini straps poke out of the tops of others. But before any of it will be allowed into the dorm room, Angie and her team will comb through every stitch of it. They've had previous experiences of an 'emergency stash' being concealed in the block heel of a boot or the lining of a padded bra.

Another patient, Laura, is watching this. She's from Pontiac, Illinois. She got into drugs aged fifteen. She was a basketball star in high school but had a row with a teammate one day and quit the team. By her own admission, she started hanging around with 'the wrong crowd', people who were actively using, and so she just started 'drinking and drugging'. 'The more I did, the more I didn't have to feel the pain.'

She said drugs were very easy to find in Chicago (a city President Trump has referred to as being 'worse than some of the places we read about in the Middle East where you have wars going on').

'You could get anything on the streets there,' says Laura. 'They don't care about you. They just care about making their money. So it was very easy.'

She says she used to steal from her parents too, taking their pills just to try them. She was miserable and wanted something to numb the pain.

Boredom and unhappiness drove her to drugs. A lack of facilities for or engagement with young people. The coroner in Stark County has to use a trailer for a morgue; the Mayor in Piketon is getting excited about a drug-sniffing dog; a church group in Pike County is taking care of its drug addicts because the wait for rehab is too long and the cost too high. The common theme – no resources. No money from central government.

This is where the 'forgotten middle' comes from – or 'the Silent Majority', as Donald Trump calls it. People who feel left behind by the federal government often have good reason for feeling that way. And who do they blame? Barack Obama.

Mayor Billy Spencer in Piketon, a Democratic area, predicted a Trump victory when we met just a few weeks before the election: 'In this part of the state, we haven't seen a whole lot of benefit for the last eight years from Barack Obama. I think a lot of people see Hillary as an extension and a continuation of some of his policies. Trump says things so I think people are saying, "Let's give him a chance."' And they did.

In Pike County, 66.1 per cent of voters picked Donald Trump, compared with 49.3 per cent who voted for Republican candidate Mitt Romney in 2012.

Ohio is a true swing state: it flips and flops between Republicans and Democrats. Only once since 1944 have Ohioans not voted for the person who ultimately became president. That was in 1960 when they voted for Richard Nixon over John F. Kennedy.

In 2016 it was a case of game, set and match. Despite the state governor's reservations, Trump won this state with a margin of eight percentage points – the biggest winning margin any candidate had scored in Ohio since George H.W. Bush in 1988.

For those working in law enforcement or drug addiction, or for the families directly affected by the opioid epidemic here, who have seen a loved one die or become estranged, President Trump is doing what he promised them he would. In March 2017, just two months into office, he signed an executive order establishing the President's Commission on Combating Drug Addiction and the Opioid Crisis. The commission is headed by New Jersey Governor Chris Christie. He is not from one of the states most impacted by the current epidemic, but nevertheless he has been tasked with finding a solution.

Barack Obama, for his part, had asked the Republican-led Congress for $1 billion for drug-treatment facilities in late 2016, but it wasn't approved.

People in this region, across the whole of Appalachia and further afield, fighting the heroin epidemic have had enough. When they viewed traditional politicians as having failed them, they looked at a businessman from New York and, in the words of the former pill-popping preacher's wife turned addiction counsellor, 'he was worth a chance'.

THE COAL MINER'S DAUGHTER'S SOLAR PANELS

'The Little Town that International Harvester Coal Miners and Their Families Built' is the catchy slogan on the sign that greets you as you pull into Benham, Kentucky. In red, white and black, the sign also bears a sketch of a coal miner with his pickaxe, leaving no doubt whatsoever as to the stock-in-trade of this town, perched as it is on the edge of Black Mountain.

Some of my favourite things about travelling across America, particularly to the lesser known sites, are the wonderful signs that you spot as you enter the various towns and townlands. Even the state signs are good for a photo collection. Some are fancy; some are plain. When you cross any state line into Kentucky you'll be treated to a particularly good one – 'Welcome to Kentucky: Unbridled Spirit'; the 'cky' of the Kentucky forms the body of a horse with its head coming out of the top of the 'y' and its mane and tail effectively blowing back across the sign. And lest you forget, the tagline is always 'Birthplace of Abraham Lincoln'.

The highest point in Kentucky is Black Mountain. Its summit is 1,263 metres (4,145 feet) above sea level and is located in Harlan County, as is Benham. You can probably guess why it's called Black Mountain – yes, there is coal in them there hills. The nearby town of Lynch, Kentucky, in its heyday, was one of the biggest coal-mining towns in the US. And according to local community action group Kentuckians for the Commonwealth, it was the 'largest coal camp in the world' by the end of the Second World War.

The mountain is also the natural habitat of the black bear, so caution is required if straying off the beaten path. It belongs to Penn-Virginia Coal – one of the few state high points to be privately owned – but a permit can be obtained to gain access.

At the height of the industrial era, 10,000 people lived in this area around Black Mountain. But with mechanisation and surface mining replacing underground human miners, plus a move away from fossil fuels, the jobs and the population declined sharply. Harlan County has lost one-third of its population in the last thirty years. Its unemployment rate is almost double the rate for the United States as a whole.

Now the region looks to tourism to help it survive. In the Kentucky Coal Mining Museum visitors can learn all about its history – no part of which is shied away from. Visitors can overnight in the School House Inn, which was the 'white school', and they can imbibe at the Eastern Kentucky Social Club, located in the next town over in the building that was home to the 'black school'.

A preserved mine – Mine 31 – gives an authentic experience of what the job of a miner involved. On top of the entrance are the words 'Safety The First Consideration Mine No 31 1920'. And while the men working here saw that every day, and safety was always considered, that does not mean mining was safe. In the 1900s, it's estimated that around 2,500 miners died across the United States every year – many here in Eastern Kentucky, as it experienced a mining boom. And it remains a precarious job: in the last thirty years 445 miners have been killed in Kentucky.

The Kentucky Coal Mining Museum was originally built as a large four-floor general store in 1927 by the Wisconsin Steel company, the parent company of International Harvester – the company that gets a mention on the sign at the edge of town.

Theresa Osbourne is the local folklorist and oral historian. She's the Appalachian programme facilitator at Southeast Kentucky Community and Technical College and also teaches some courses at the Western Kentucky University, and she works as co-curator at the Kentucky Coal Mining Museum. She's a member of the Kentucky Oral History Commission. She is the foremost expert on coal mining and the history of Southeastern Kentucky. Born and raised in Central Kentucky, she moved east to the mountains nearly thirty years ago and loves it.

'There was nothing that you might want that you could not get at that company store. They had furniture, they had clothes, they had food, they had televisions, appliances, knick-knacks and candy, and they had a soda fountain so that the kids could come in after school or on Saturdays. They could come in to the soda fountain and share an ice-cream and then buy them a bag of candy for 25 cents, walk across the street to the movie theatre and get in there for a dime. They had a whole day of entertainment.'

Back when the mines were booming, the trend was for the mining companies to build 'coal camps' where the workers and their families would live. Here on the edge of Black Mountain, Wisconsin Steel arrived around 1910 and bought the mineral rights. They started a coal camp and called it Benham. A short distance away us Steel came in and did the same and called it Lynch.

Theresa explains that 'in the early days of coal mining, the coal camp was sort of the way that coal mining companies worked it. They would come into an area and they wanted their workers all to be in one spot. So they would build communities. I've got a map from the 1930s – 1935, something like that – where it shows the number of coal camps that were in Harlan County and there were like fifty or sixty, all over this county. They would come in, they would build a community, they would build houses and schools. They would build churches, medical facilities, pretty much everything that the residents would need to be a self-contained community. Some of them … were what they called "model coal camps". They were sort of the commercial for the idea of coal-camp life.'

Benham and nearby Lynch were the gold standard of coal camps. They were known as 'captive coal camps' and so they fared a little better than most during the Great Depression. The coal in this area was not sold on the open market but was mined as a resource to be transported by railroad back up the country to Pennsylvania and Wisconsin. In Benham in particular they produced coal and coke. The coke from Benham and Lynch would be used in the steel-processing plants – the steel-processing plants that now lie vacant further north in Pennsylvania, in the same steel communities that Donald Trump has promised to bring the steel jobs back to, as he's promising here to bring back the coal jobs.

The International Harvester company had a large plant making farm machinery in Chicago. The coal from here was used to produce steel for the manufacture of, as Theresa says, 'International trucks, or farm equipment, ploughs, the cultivators, the tractors.'

She is very proud of this history. 'If you kind of trace it back, it's so cool that a coal camp in Kentucky helped to provide the energy to create all this farm equipment and then it could be sold out into Wisconsin into the Grain Belt. And so we helped to feed the nation by providing for that energy to produce that steel.'

It also helps to illustrate the full-circle story of coal mining in Kentucky, the steel processing in Pennsylvania and the farmers in Wisconsin.

Money is really tight in this part of Kentucky in Appalachia. As in the entire region, jobs have dried up. According to the Appalachia Regional Commission, the area lost nearly 10,500 coal-mining jobs in 2016 alone. Between 2011 and 2016, a total of 33,500 coal-mining jobs disappeared. Donald Trump told people in these areas repeatedly that he loved coal. 'Big beautiful coal' was how he frequently described it. He promised to 'bring back the jobs'. The people living in this area know the coal jobs are not coming back. They don't feel the same as those in Pennsylvania pining for steel plants or those in the auto trade in Michigan. Those jobs were manufacturing jobs. Manufacturing still takes place and always will – it's just a question of where.

But mining is different. It involves, for starters, a finite resource, and those who live here know that the environment must be protected and that fossil fuels are not as popular as they once were. And they're OK with that. Any jobs would be good – they don't have to be mining jobs.

There's no mining in Benham now; there was a little in Lynch for a while, but not recently. Theresa is blunt about the situation in this corner of Appalachia, despite promises of 'big beautiful coal' jobs from the president.

'We have been hard hit with a lot of loss of coal jobs in the last eight years. And we look forward to the possibility, you know, if any jobs come our way, we will welcome them. There is the hope that there will be some new mining jobs, but nobody's saying, "Oh yeah, we're gonna."'

She says they read about the economic recovery that has supposedly occurred since the financial collapse of 2008, but the trickle-down of that hasn't been felt in this part of the world. And although the local people may not actually think coal jobs can come back as the president promises, they're keeping an open mind.

'I think that this area has been in such partnership with coal for so many years, that any time that they hear that there's a possibility of coal jobs returning, that is always looked forward to with anticipation. However, coal being what coal is … it is a boom and bust kind of cycle that it has gone through over the years. So our local area is also looking at diversifying their economic base. We're looking into heritage tourism, which the Kentucky Coal Museum is a part of. They've got a zip line. They're doing some ATV trails and tracks because we have such beautiful mountains … this is a commodity that we have that's very special and very unique. And so we're trying to advertise ourselves and put it out there that you can come here and you can stay in cabins. People are building cabins and things like that.'

Kentucky has been a swing state in the past but in recent election cycles has swung firmly Republican. Population-wise, there are more registered Democrats here than Republicans, but many of those Democrats are Republican leaning. Kentuckians voted for Jimmy Carter and Bill Clinton twice, but they have voted solidly Republican since then. In fact, Donald Trump's performance in this state in 2016 was the strongest Republican performance for decades. He got almost twice the vote that Clinton did, winning every single county except two – Jefferson County, where the city of Louisville is, and Fayette County, where the city of Lexington is located.

Although Trump won the state with 62.5 per cent and a 30-point victory margin, in many counties he won well over 80 per cent of the vote. Here in Harlan County he garnered 84.9 per cent. That's an increase on Mitt Romney (81.2 per cent), John McCain (72 per cent) and George W. Bush (77 per cent). So it's hard to argue against the fact that his message resonated particularly well here.

But, Theresa stresses, despite the positive outlook, things are 'pretty bad'; no new industry has come in to replace the coal mines.

'We have been in the middle of a pretty severe economic crisis, officially, in Harlan County, we were very hard hit. We have seen a massive amount of people who have left the county to go find jobs in other places. That's one of the things that happens … over the years we have lost a lot of our population, just because of the way things work.'

She's a realist, though. She says all of the folks around here are. They know the mining jobs aren't coming back. Mining is over.

'This has been happening since the beginning of coal mining. It wasn't related to politics. It was just related to the progression and technology improvement that, as we move along, we have the need of fewer and fewer actual hands on to do that work. It was not one thing. It was not one person, one thing. It was a combination of a lot of different things that have hit all at the same time to make this perfect storm of … Causing the loss of jobs.'

But nobody has spoken to that issue for some time. When Barack Obama was running for the presidency in 2008, he struggled in this area. Hillary Clinton beat him here in the Democratic primary by a margin of three to one. When it came to the two-man race with John McCain, Obama all but pulled his campaign from this state, realising it would no doubt be solidly red and so not worth the expenditure. As a result, many people here never really felt a connection to him. Donald Trump was a different endeavour entirely, frequently holding rallies and speaking to the issues that counted.

There is great hope for what Trump might achieve for the communities here, ravaged by the job losses. But they are trying to help themselves too, something Theresa puts down to the Appalachian blood in their veins.

'There is hope that there will be something that will come from the government, but they're also … We are Appalachians. And one of the things the Appalachian people, as a group, they came in here and this was the wide-open plains. This was the wild west of the very early colonies of America. And they came in and they carved out, you know, homes and communities out of this wilderness, and they figured out how to do things. And so we still have those people. There are some who say, "Well, if we could get a government programme in here," and then there are some that say, "Well, let's figure out on our own what we can do for ourselves."'

They don't have a great reliance on the federal government intervening, but the local politicians are doing what they can, she says.

'Our county government realises that we have to start looking and working on being proactive to develop some diversity in our economic base. I'm sure that they – I don't know this because I'm not political, I'm just one of the little peons that goes to work and does her job every day. But I know that, I'm pretty sure I feel confident that, our county government is out there looking for people to come and get factories in here. But at the same time, they're also developing the heritage tourism and the nature trails and ATV trails and that kind of thing. I think they're even creating a horseback trail along the top of Pine Mountain, which is one of the mountains that is located in Harlan County.'

While the town's focus has always been on the coal-rich Black Mountain, that other mountain, Pine Mountain, which can't be mined due to its geological structure, provides fertile farmland.

Kentucky is one of the American states that is most visually like Ireland – green fields and hills, with a limestone bedrock that makes the grass particularly good for horses. It's no wonder the city of Lexington, the horse-industry capital of the US, is twinned with County Kildare.

There is a strong tradition of farming here in Harlan County. When the mines were in their heyday, some just mined, some just farmed and some did a bit of both.

With the downturn, the economic collapse, the poverty, the food shortages, many people have taken to farming on a small scale. Theresa herself now keeps eleven goats at her house. Her son has goats as well and a high tunnel for produce in his backyard. They availed of those through a project called Grow Appalachia, which has been worked out through a sort of partnership with local health clinics and hospitals and various other local agencies. So many people in the region were on food stamps and weren't getting fresh vegetables and good food that Grow Appalachia was born from necessity. Now there's a farmers' market where the community buy and sell and barter with each other.

Theresa explains that because there is a 'background of growing our own food', this project provided 'help and assistance, seeds and tools and things like that, to help the local people begin to start growing their own food again'. Like her family, many people are raising goats; others are raising chickens.

She stresses that this programme is not a 'big government' initiative. It is something the local community is doing, with the help of some state grants and a major donation from a philanthropist. John Paul DeJoria, the billionaire environmentalist, philanthropist and co-founder of the Paul Mitchell haircare and Patrón Tequila brands, started Grow Appalachia in 2010. In its first six years, the project produced nearly 810,000 kilogrammes of fresh food. It states its aim as follows: 'Grow Appalachia emphasises food production in order to introduce as much no-cost, fresh, healthy food as possible to the region.' This not-for-profit non-governmental organisation is operating (and needed) in the middle of one of the wealthiest countries on earth, not in a neglected area in a developing or 'third world' country.

The youth of the area are focused on future-proofing their employment prospects. Theresa's grandson is involved in a programme run in conjunction with the Interapt technology company and the Shaping Our Appalachian Region (SOAR) initiative that teaches coding and computer science to young people.

So the area born out of hard labour and mining is looking to technology for its future.

And as if to echo that, something that at first look appears to suggest the universe is laughing at coal-mining communities and officially signalling the end of days, something else dramatic, is going on here in Benham.

The Kentucky Coal Mining Museum is getting solar panels.

It's not a joke. The museum is having its entire roof covered with them. The complete project, when finished, will generate 60 kilowatts of electricity. The museum built to honour the tradition of mining for fossil fuels is being turned into a small solar-power plant for the town of Benham. It will feed into the local grid and help power not just the museum but also a good portion of the town. It's part of a bigger initiative that, when finished, will generate 250 kilowatts of solar power, so the town will be completely self-sufficient. Everything in the Little Town that International Harvester Coal Miners and Their Families Built will be run on energy generated by the almost year-round sunshine.

Tre Sexton is the owner of Bluegrass Solar, the company charged with the project. Tre was working with his father until recently in his car dealership and real-estate business. His father is a rather prescient fellow and a few years ago, when he saw the decline in fossil fuels, thought about getting into the renewable-energy business. But his dad sat on the idea for a few years, and eventually Tre asked him if he was going to do anything about it, and if not, would he mind if Tre did? That was mid-2016. By early 2017 they already had eighteen workers and the contract for the museum. By late 2017, they employed another twelve, such was the demand for business. Tre has gone from working for his father to employing thirty people in about eighteen months.

Tre is modest about the project and his own entrepreneurial endeavours.

'It's a pretty interesting story, isn't it? Well, it's really just to save money, though. They found themselves in a good position and it really just seemed like a logical economic move.'

The 'they' he is referring to is the museum and its patrons – the Southeast Community and Technical College. Tre explains how they're about to lose a lot of funding for various programmes according to the Trump administration's budget and they needed to come up with a way to keep the lights on. Literally.

Tre says the college is 'facing lay-offs and all sorts of bad stuff so they had to do something to cut down on these costs and the first target would be something like museums. It's one of those fringe things that they just happen to oversee.'

Given how the mining history is so key to the community and forms the backbone of their new economic plans to attract tourists, nobody wanted to see the museum close down.

Tre says the museum was an ideal candidate for solar panels, as it has a flat roof. 'It'll be, in essence, a mini power plant.' Benham has its own independent power board and isn't reliant on one of the big national providers – if it can produce its own energy, it can move away from the more expensive commercial providers.

In addition to the museum, Tre's company will be installing panels on 'a few municipal buildings and one private business'. Putting some solar panels in a nearby park and the local Little League field is also under consideration. The project for the area is ambitious.

Tre estimates once all the solar panels are installed it will dramatically reduce what the town is buying from coal-fired plants in the area, and 'it's going to cut the cost to the city and the power board by, we're hoping, over 50 per cent at least'.

He says that as the communities have become more interested in growing their own food, they've become more environmentally aware and renewable energy sources are really piquing their interest. Tre has been receiving queries from neighbouring communities, and that is why the business is growing and creating jobs at a reasonably rapid rate.

But he's under no illusions. While environmental concerns play a part, the relentless economic squeeze of the last eight years or so is the driver. 'I would say that no municipality, unless they're a very lucky one, probably find themselves in a great economic situation right now, so anywhere where they can find an avenue to cut costs is gonna be helpful to them, and energy just so happens, most of the time, to be their principal expense.'

Tre is not as quick to blame the Obama administration for the financial situation as some others here.

'It's certainly come as manifest of a snowball effect of actions taken in legislature and federal government but, over the happenings of eight years, who could say what was the trigger?'

While Tre now has a vested interest in a push towards renewables and a move away from fossil fuels, he is still a local Kentuckian and understands the pain the loss of the coal-industry jobs has caused. Just like Theresa, he's willing to give the Trump administration a chance to make a difference. Even though he doesn't necessarily think the coal jobs can be brought back, the messaging is welcome.

'It's kinda bold to say but a lot of the fossil fuels are just crossing themselves out. People are just finding it to be a more economically viable option to go with the renewables, especially for the sorts of places we're targeting, like civic buildings, municipalities, large commercial interests, things like that. A lot of the power companies around here are just going crazy with additional fees and add-ons and things. What your actual energy costs is only about half the bill. Half of it's just nonsense fees.'

But when all of the Kentucky Coal Mining Museum's panels are up and running, it should provide at least 90 per cent of the museum's power needs. In ninety years the building will have gone from being a general store in a model, purpose-built town for coal miners to a solar-powered museum safeguarding that mining history for a town teaching its young people to become computer scientists.

While the spirits are a little higher in this part of Appalachia, the outlook a little brighter, the recent past has been hard, the burden of a sustained financial struggle not easily forgotten. While Hillary Clinton came bringing a liberal message of inclusivity and the collective good, Donald Trump brought one of individual improvements. His message hit home here, as across Appalachia. They had tried 'the rest': here was someone new, someone who was in tune with their concerns, who recognised them and at least said he would try to do something about them, even if they know themselves that nothing can be done. The coal-mining days are over. As local historian Theresa put it, nobody is 'sitting here waiting and counting on the possibility of coal jobs'.

Virginia

THE RED WOMEN OF POWHATAN COUNTY

'Ta-da!' says Thelma Allen, pulling her copy of the US constitution from her handbag. She carries it with her everywhere. Jean pipes up, 'I have mine out in my briefcase in the car.' Thelma checks the back of hers. 'Oh, this is a special one. These are the ones we handed out at that Republican meeting – do you remember?' They all nod over their lattes, iced teas and hot teas. Of course they remember. For these are the Republican Women of Powhatan County. Red and proud.

They're having coffee in the Italian Delight bistro. It's cute in an American strip mall sort of way. In a loose interpretation of a Venetian ristorante, there's a deli at the front with wedges of Italian meats, glass slab trays of fresh homemade tiramisu and jars of olives. There are plastic olive decorations too and bottles of wine. Lots of bottles of wine. The owner is Nino Bussa. A friendly man, a Sicilian immigrant, he repeatedly offers food and drinks.

Italian Delight is located on the romantically named South Creek Route. There's nothing terribly romantic about that street in reality, though. It's a dual carriageway. Set back from it is the village of Powhatan itself. Now, *it* is romantic – small and compact and quaint, wooden porches and decks, full of well-preserved civil-war-era buildings. There's a courthouse and a library, a post office and a town hall and a funky cafe-cum-bookshop that serves an excellent warm-the-cockles chilli.

The women meet at the Italian Delight once a week to discuss Republican Party affairs as members of the Mill Quarter Republican Women's Club. Their chairperson is Jean Gannon, a highly organised and driven woman.

The county has a population of 28,000. Virginia itself is a swing state, as purple as they come. The northern part of the state, nearest Washington DC, tends to vote largely Democratic. It's home to some of the wealthiest districts in the country, essentially suburbs of DC, where many Washingtonian workers live.

Virginia is, of course, birthplace of the nation's first president, George Washington. He was born in Westmoreland County on his father Augustine's plantation. His father's first wife – and the mother to three of his children – died at a young age. Augustine later remarried and had six more children – their first born being George, the future president. Augustine Washington moved the whole family up state to another plantation, known today as Mount Vernon. George's father died when he was eleven, and that dramatically changed the course of George's education and, ultimately, his life.

One of the famous quotes attributed to George Washington is 'I cannot tell a lie', and in this era of lies and 'alternative facts' and 'truths' that are not true, it has proved fodder for many a comic.

Here's how the historians of Mount Vernon Estate relay the myth of the cherry tree, drawing on the work of Washington's biographer Mason Locke Weems and his *Life of Washington*.

'The cherry tree myth is the most well-known and longest enduring legend about George Washington. In the original story, when Washington was six years old he received a hatchet as a gift and damaged his father's cherry tree. When his father discovered what he had done, he became angry and confronted him. Young George bravely said, "I cannot tell a lie ... I did cut it with my hatchet." Washington's father embraced him and rejoiced that his son's honesty was worth more than a thousand trees.'[14]

But actually, George Washington's most famous quote is a lie, a myth made up by Mason Locke Weems after Washington's death to fill in some missing details from his childhood and to give some colour to the book. Indeed, it could be argued to be the first 'alternative fact', an expression initially used by Donald Trump's communications adviser Kellyanne Conway in an interview with Chuck Todd on MSNBC's Sunday political show *Meet the Press*.

So here in a state filled with civil war landmarks and memorials, revolutionary George Washington is a bit of a poster boy – literally. His image is everywhere, in posters and paintings – some respectful, some not so much. One diner in Richmond, the state capital, has a chalk sketch of him on their blackboard. But he's been Trump-ised. He's wearing a 'Make Metallica Great Again' baseball cap, and a speech bubble comes from his mouth. But instead of saying 'I cannot tell a lie', it says 'I cannot tell an alternative fact'.

But that's in the area around DC. Further south it's a very different place – a different landscape and different people.

Southern Virginia is rural, farming is the industry and in a place like Powhatan County the vast majority of the population identify as Republican. It holds the title of the 'reddest county in Virginia'. In 2012, although Virginia voted for Obama overall, 72.4 per cent of the voters in the Powhatan area voted for Mitt Romney – the biggest Republican turnout in the state of Virginia. In 2016 these ladies were adamant that they would win that accolade once again.

This time, 70.38 per cent of the voters in Powhatan County voted for Trump (11,885 people), with an overall turnout of 85.93 per cent. Voting matters in this area. In fact, the Virginia Electoral Board Association gave the citizens of Powhatan County a special award for having the highest voter turnout in any county in Virginia at the 2016 elections.

But they didn't win the prize for giving Trump his greatest majority in Virginia in 2016. They were beaten by a little county in the southwestern corner of Virginia, bordering West Virginia in the Appalachian Mountains. There, 81.97 per cent of the electorate picked Trump. The name of that area? The very un-Trump-like, non-'tremendously'-named Bland County.[15]

This particular morning, in the Italian Delight restaurant, the Republican women are discussing what makes a good president. It's a given, of course, that in the election year of 2016 there is only one answer to that question for them, and it doesn't include a list of adjectives like strong, intelligent, good decision-maker, fair-minded, etc. It's just a one-word answer: 'Trump'.

This Tuesday, the women are buzzing. The past weekend they had held an extremely successful fundraiser for a local congressional candidate who is fighting for a seat in one of the down-ballot races. They had a pot-luck community party – a grand-scale version of what I remember from my Dublin childhood as a 'street party' or have attended in Washington DC as a 'block party'. Everyone brings food and there's face-painting and games for the children. People bring seats and tables and sit around and eat and drink and chat, and in this case donate money. Only here in Powhatan, it was in a field that a Republican member had kindly donated the use of. About a hundred people came; they had lunch for everyone and lots of horses – and of course speeches. And it raised enough money to continue their campaign efforts right through election day. They ran out of Trump campaign materials at one stage so they held another fundraiser to enable them to have extra signs, stickers and banners made.

These women are hard-core Republicans. They care about the party; they care about the party's values. And they want to make sure their president does too.

According to chairperson Jean Gannon, 'I think the American people are pretty much fed up with what goes in our government. Being both the Republican and the Democrat side. There is a level of corruption in Congress and Donald Trump doesn't have a filter. He's saying what a lot of people are thinking and he gets ridiculed for that by the press. But the American people love it. I think he's doing a great job.'

She adds with laughter, 'And in New York you say what's on your mind!'

Historical documents show that the US Founding Fathers put great effort into designing the executive branch of United States government – whether it should be one person or a council and how much power they should have.

Much of that discussion took place on 1 June 1787 in the assembly room of the State House in Philadelphia. All of the delegates to the federal convention were there – forty-three men from eleven of the thirteen states (Rhode Island boycotted the convention over fears their interests would not be well looked after and New Hampshire joined proceedings later). James Madison observed (he chronicled proceedings in detailed notes) that they had reached 'a point of great importance' – who should take charge over a newly created nation? (Ray Raphael sets out the to-ing and fro-ing in excellent detail in his book *Mr President: How and Why the Founders Created a Chief Executive*, Alfred A. Knopf, 2012). But ultimately discussions centred on how much power this one person would have, how they would be elected and what offences would be impeachable. They had, after all, just rejected a monarchy and did not want to return to something similar. That spirit echoed in the fears of Charles Pinckney of South Carolina: that a single person in the executive branch 'would render the Executive a monarchy, of the worst kind, to wit an elective one'.

Given the era, and that all of the negotiators were men, it is probable that it did not cross any of their minds that the leader could in fact be a woman. So the US constitution (just like the original Irish constitution drafted over 100 years later) refers to the president using the male pronoun.

In April 2017, in her first interview in public since her defeat, at a Women of the World event in New York, Hillary Clinton said that she was working on a book about the campaign, her loss and particularly how and why she did so badly among women, especially among white women – 53 per cent of people who look like her voted for Trump. Gender-studies experts tell us time and again that when it comes to hiring for a job, bosses look for someone who is like them. So if the boss is an older white guy in a grey suit, he's going to be drawn to a younger white guy in a grey suit for a junior executive job and not a young black woman in a blue dress, for example. But in the case of the female voters of the US, they didn't fit that profile. They didn't go for the person who looked like them. They went for the one who not only didn't look like them, but also was on the record for repeatedly saying and doing things that played down women and their roles. Yes, Trump and his supporters will point to his daughter and a handful of other female executives in Trump organisation as examples of how highly he thinks of women. Many often also point to this passage in his 1987 book *The Art of the Deal*: 'It's funny. My own mother was a housewife all her life. And yet it's turned out that I've hired a lot of women for top jobs, and they've been among my best people. Often, in fact, they are far more effective than the men around them.'[16]

This statement contains a compliment and a fair-minded approach; however, it is tempered by Trump's own surprise that this is in fact the case.

But regardless, there is video evidence of Donald Trump speaking freely – as he thought he was in private – boasting about how easily he could 'grab women', as on that now infamous *Access Hollywood* video tape of Trump and the show's host, Billy Bush, on a tour bus. They were discussing the woman they were about to meet to film a segment for the show, and Donald Trump said, 'I've got to use some Tic Tacs, just in case I start kissing her. You know I'm automatically attracted to beautiful – I just start kissing them. It's like a magnet. Just kiss, I don't even wait.' And then the seemingly damning line: 'When you're a star, they'll let you do it. You can do anything … Grab them by the pussy. You can do anything.'

It's not just the vulgarity of that statement that caused offence to so many: it was the insight into his view of professional women that can be read into those remarks. He had discussed Billy Bush's predecessor, TV host Nancy O'Dell, entirely from a sexual perspective. The same impression was given as Trump and Bush joked about the woman they were about to meet, Arianne Zucker. It all speaks to an attitude. It was described repeatedly as 'locker-room' bravado. And let's be honest, so the argument goes, we've all heard men speak like that about women, and to pretend otherwise would be naive at best and dishonest at worst. But voters had to ask themselves whether they wanted that guy, who seems like a guy you know from a bar or sports club, to be their president? The Democrats, and the chattering classes, assumed not. They assumed that the electorate would expect a higher level of virtue from their president. That voters would want a 'good man' who was to be placed on a pedestal. That middle-of-the-road conservative voters would be turned off by a newly married man talking about trying to 'fuck' a married woman, and that he might 'just start kissing' another woman he had never met before.

But that is not what happened. That didn't enter into the equation. And look back at history – the precedent was there. Voters picked John F. Kennedy, amidst allegations that he was a serial philanderer. Voters gave resounding support to the Democratic party in the midterm elections in 1998 – a year when the party's figurehead President Bill Clinton had been involved in a salacious scandal with White House intern Monica Lewinsky. This was the first time since 1934 that a sitting president's party had gained seats in a midterm election. Voters in America have a proven record of ignoring this sort of indiscretion. In a country where, according to Pew Research, 76.5 per cent consider themselves religious, it appears to be a case of 'Let he [or she] who is without sin cast the first stone'.

Certainly that was the viewpoint of many of the white Republican women that I met as I went around the country. I am focusing more here on white women, because the majority of white women voted for Trump, while the majority of non-white women voted for Clinton. White women had the chance to vote for the first woman President and most of those who came out to vote didn't take it.

I was interested to find out whether for those women of Powhatan, Virginia, that concept of voting for the first woman president in the nation's history appealed to them. Did they feel a sort of gender pride, like the ethnic pride that drove many African Americans to vote for Barack Obama in 2008?

Thelma Allen is a defender of the constitution. She has such patriotic spirit that today she's arrived to meet me wearing an American-flag-themed sequined blouse. She's the one carrying her constitution around in her handbag .

Thelma is so in favour of Donald Trump that ahead of the election she covered her car in Trump and Pence stickers and drove it up to her relatives in Northern Virginia, in an area that was very much anti-Trump. She left her car in their driveway for a week, refusing to move it. She really does not like Hillary Clinton.

'I could go into a very long litany about Hillary Clinton but I think her record speaks for itself. There is no way I would ever vote for somebody that has done the things that she has done. I also feel that she would be an endangerment to the country. So that's my whole theory of the thing. I think Trump offers a businessman's look at the country in a time when we need to take some action about the threats at home and abroad.'

Debbie Elam runs an animal hospital with her husband. It's that business experience that she likes about Donald Trump too. 'My husband and I own a small business and we know there's a lot of challenges with small business and if he has been able to be successful in his career then I think if the country was run more accountable then we may have a better economy as a result of that.'

The business aspect is important to all of these women. They live in a rural area but aren't reliant on farming. They're focused on their own small businesses and what can improve their lives.

Ann Tackett is younger than the others, glamorous and perfectly turned out for the coffee morning. She has two children and her responsibilities as their mother, as well her own career interests, are the main factors motivating her when she chooses who to vote for. Her husband is a police officer.

'As a woman, I don't know how you could support Hillary Clinton. I'm pro-life, I have children, small children that are in the public schools. They don't necessarily always feel safe and I think that the last eight years has made my family not feel safe and I feel that he can bring back some of the order that is missing and that has changed in the last eight years. I'm looking forward to the repeal of the Obamacare that has killed our small businesses. I'm pro-police, and I feel that he is as well.'

The repeal of Obamacare is something that most Republicans seeking election or re-election ran on in 2016. And in 2014 and in 2012. During the Obama administration, they passed several bills calling for its repeal – some ended up on the president's desk, all of which were voted. Donald Trump swore repealing it would be the first thing he did on coming into office   along with deporting two million illegal immigrants. It was the first bill that he and his Republican Party colleagues on Capitol Hill tried to get passed, but they failed utterly, ultimately withdrawing the bill before putting it to a vote on the House floor because they knew they would not have the votes to get it passed.

Thelma agrees that he will 'bring law and order back to our country'. Although Powhatan is a small town, they don't feel that removed from the rioting and violence they've seen in other parts of the country, she says. 'I've been a little concerned with all the things we're seeing on TV lately, the riots in the street et cetera, et cetera. He is talking about things like the community, how to help the communities become better. Our educational system. He's hitting on a lot of the hot buttons that are necessary to be addressed, especially in this day and age. I have children, I have grandchildren and I have great-grandchildren. They're all going to be affected by what he does and I just really believe that he does have a plan and that he cares about the people and we just need to see that he has the platform so that everybody understands exactly what he's talking about.'

And talking about law and order leads to the inevitable discussion about the second-amendment right – commonly referred to as the right to bear arms. Or in its full form: 'A well regulated Militia, being necessary to the security of a free State, the right of the people to keep and bear Arms, shall not be infringed.'

For Debbie, this is one of the main reasons she picked Donald Trump over Hillary Clinton, as she explains: 'our country was founded on the basic principles of our forefathers and to me personally second-amendment rights is very important to all citizens of this country'.

She tells me that 'getting rid of the guns' would have been top of Hillary Clinton's agenda. 'I would not be surprised if she had brought trucks through and confiscated firearms.'

She takes very seriously the right of people who are able 'to arm themselves responsibly'. 'I'm not talking about the criminals, I'm talking about the law-abiding citizens who know the laws on concealed carry, who know the laws about what they can and can't do. In this country you can't brandish a firearm: that is a felony. You will go to jail if you wave a firearm. And somebody that's responsible knows how important that is not to do. It's the people that don't follow the laws that cause the problems.'

She feels very strongly about any threat to remove her weapons from her – particularly because she has a shooting range in her front garden. She designed and constructed it herself. A neighbour with a digger helped her fashion a trough and a mound. She often has her girlfriends around for target practice. They usually call the local sheriff to be on hand too so he can keep watch on things. She described their gatherings to me as like a book club but with guns...

She is convinced that the liberals have a plan to get rid of guns altogether. 'I think it would start slow and then continue to grow,' she says. 'Maybe they would start to limit the availability of ammunition, maybe certain firearms, maybe the automatic firearms, maybe they would start eliminating those. But I think there is a plan to limit our second-amendment rights.' She is not going to let that happen.

The other issue they all have strong opinions on is immigration – notwithstanding the fact that all of their ancestors were immigrants. Some know the heritage, others don't. Ellen Nau says her family hailed from Ireland, Germany and England. Those living in the Appalachian region have mixed ancestry. It was a prime location for the earliest settlers, so many can trace their roots to the Scots Irish who arrived before the big immigration wave around the time of the Great Irish Famine. But large numbers of English and Welsh, and German and Portuguese, settled there too and, of course, the Native Americans lived there before all of the settlers arrived.

The Appalachian region has far more white people, proportionally, than in most other parts of the country. White people make up 62.3 per cent of the US population as a whole; in this region it's 82.5 per cent.

While Powhatan is not a poor area, it's not one of the gold-plated districts in Virginia either. But the homes are larger and the facilities are better than those on the other side of Appalachia. Donald Trump was born into wealth and has lived his life in wealth. Time and again this fact raises the question of how he can be viewed as an 'everyman' by so many.

Thelma Allen, the constitution-carrying grandmother, has a theory. She explains that he complains repeatedly about how bad the tax structure is in the US, but he made it his business to find out to best use it to his advantage, that's how he got to be so wealthy. 'The tax structure is what's holding people back.' People believe that if they could get a handle on their own affairs the way Donald Trump has, they'd be better off. 'I think the man has a depth that we haven't seen and I'd like to see more of it.'

But this group of Republican power women surely have an opinion on Trump's attitude to women. They are all articulate, opinionated and strong willed and most have more than a hint of a feminist streak.

Ann is forceful in her defence of Donald Trump. She sums up perfectly, to my mind, why women like Trump, how they can see past his low-grade talk and want him as president. And this is possibly the moment when I realised that Donald Trump stood a very good chance of winning.

A friend of hers was chatting about another plus point of Trump's when Ann said, 'You know, when I'm going to vote, I'm not voting for the president for marital advice. Or how to raise my children. Or for spiritual guidance. I'm voting for him to run the country. To put the right people in place. I have a priest for my spiritual needs, you know. So we're not electing him for those reasons. We need him to run the country.'

Jean chimed in: 'Yes. His leadership.'

Then Thelma brought up the other common justification for woman who like Trump: his family. 'We have seen them paraded all throughout the TV and they're a marvellous looking group of people. They're well spoken, they're well mannered, they're everything that we would want for our family. And if he can raise his children that way, I think he can do the same thing for the country. He can set things in place that our children will profit from too.'

And we're back to the American Dream again: the singular focus on making sure you give your children a better station in life than you had yourself.

So in addition to the Powhatan women liking Trump's leadership and his family, they also liked his energy. They spoke about Trump in the same way we'd heard people talk about Barack Obama eight years previously.

Debbie explains, 'We do believe that he can bring the change that we have much needed in this country. Optimism, hope and a future, a brighter future.' She adds, 'And to give America some excitement.'

The issue of least concern to these women is that Donald Trump was the only presidential candidate ever who did not release their tax returns ahead of the election. This issue drove US media commentators and Democrats apoplectic. What was he hiding? How much tax did he pay? How much did he give to charity? How many loans did he have and what about foreign holdings?

Being Republican conservative women, the group tends towards the belief that Americans are forced to pay too much tax as it is, that there is too much interference by 'big government', and so not one of them cares at all about Donald Trump's tax returns. But the issue of taxation in general gets them very animated.

As Jean says, 'We're all over-taxed as it is, so if we can get somebody in there that can maybe reform the tax laws, wouldn't that be fantastic?' And she brings it back to one of their core concerns – the military. 'The whole taxing system started as a way to support our military – it's based on the safety of the citizens in this country.'

Thelma – the grandmother who carries the constitution in her handbag – says funding the military is a hot-button issue for her. 'There has not been enough money going to fund the military. We need the military. We need to support them. We need to fund them. Donald Trump is a man who is invested in the constitution.'

Jean interjects, 'And now look at what we pay in taxes and where that money goes! I've got really great ideas on how to spend my own money. I don't need a congressman or senator to tell me how to do it!'

She used to run a small business herself. 'If Donald Trump has a way of conducting his business and getting more money to his employees and making profits in his business rather than being taxed, well, my hat's off to him!'

Ellen Nau points to the situation of the American multinationals located in Ireland and other European countries with more favourable tax regimes than the one available to them in the US. 'They're doing business there because they don't want to be over-taxed. If any of us make a loss in our retirement portfolio, we take that loss off our income tax.' She doesn't see any difference in them doing that and Donald Trump using loopholes to write off almost a billion dollars against one year of his tax returns.

These ladies don't care about ever seeing his tax return, let alone what's in it.

'Nobody cares about my tax return,' says Debbie.

'Yeah,' says Jean. 'I would never ask Deb about hers, or Thelma or Ann or Ellen. I would never ask how much they pay in taxes.'

And Ann says, 'Personally, when I file my taxes any time I can use a deduction, I take it. And so it would be the same if I was a businessman. If there was a loophole or a deduction that I could take, I would take it. So part of that is just his good business sense.'

While the Red Women of Powhatan County don't take offence at Donald Trump's lack of tax transparency, or his comments on women, they took great offence when Hillary Clinton referred to Trump supporters as belonging in 'a basket of deplorables'. This much-quoted remark came from a speech she delivered in New York on September 9th 2016 at an LGBT for Hillary gala. 'To just be grossly generalistic, you could put half of Trump's supporters into what I call the basket of deplorables. Right? The racist, sexist, homophobic, xenophobic, Islamaphobic – you name it. And unfortunately there are people like that. And he has lifted them up.'

Debbie explains their anger. 'I don't think any of us here are deplorable. I think we're all smart women. We take care of our families, we have jobs, we're responsible for our actions. I don't think she was very responsible when she profiled Republican men and women as being deplorable. I was never thinking of voting for her anyway, but that was really awful. I don't see how that is much different than the comments Donald Trump made. But it's kind of … been left to go away … but yet Donald Trump's comments are on every station, every day. I just feel that there's a double standard for her. She's allowed to get away with things and statements that she's making and Donald Trump is not being given the same courtesies from the media.'

Ironically, Hillary Clinton supporters often complained about just the opposite, that the US media was too harsh on her. Nobody's ever satisfied with the job the media does. The first amendment protects the freedom of the press, alongside freedom of religion, and that's something else the women think is under threat: an inalienable right that is causing an uprising.

The last word to Thelma. 'I think that the people have finally woken up that we're having a basic erosion of rights in this country – not only the gun rights but also your religious rights. I know that there was some statement by Hillary Clinton that the churches were just going to have to change their positions. Well, that right is being threatened and just your general erosion of society. Public schools aren't what they used to be. It's just law enforcement under attack. So I think these are the concerns of the basic population and would override perhaps some of the endorsements of what we would call elitists, or higher-up politicians, and I think it's the basic movement across the board as recognised by Bernie Sanders on the Democrat side, whose philosophies we would not support but, again, appealed to a basic uprising of people and voters and the Democratic Party.

So, I think it's just an overriding concern about the state of the country.' A country in such 'a state' that only a non-politician, an experienced, accomplished businessperson, can help. America is in such a state that only Donald Trump can fix it.

North Carolina

HOLIDAYMAKERS SPLASH AS LOCAL CHILDREN GO HUNGRY

B uckets and spades. Blow-up beds and barbecues. Kayaks and paddle-boards. Barefoot and T-shirt-less. Welcome to the beach.

The North Carolina Outer Banks are home to some of the most glorious beaches in the United States. They're a group of barrier islands that lean out like a hook off the coast of North Carolina, jutting into the Atlantic Ocean, separating the mainland from the powerful body of water, next stop Morocco. One of the islands, Roanoke, was the site of England's first settlement in the New World, a mission sponsored by Sir Walter Raleigh, whose name lives on in the city of Raleigh, North Carolina – although here it's pronounced 'raw-lee' rather than the 'rally' pronunciation used in Ireland and the UK.

The Outer Banks offer something for everyone. At the risk of sounding like a cheesy travel advert, it's really quite a glorious spot. If almost everyone wasn't speaking English with an American accent, you could quite easily be in any top holiday hotspot in any paradise beach location in the world. There are upscale resorts with restaurants with white linen tablecloths, where jackets and shoes are required for dinner. There are sand-filled food joints, where a bathing suit and flip-flops are appropriate attire, where you can quite literally paddle your own canoe right up to the table. Then there are small villages where self-catering is the only option, renting a two- or three-storey wooden home built on sticks to cope with rising tides, with outdoor showers to keep the sand out of the house, fish-gutting tables in the yard to prep your haul and hammocks and hot-tubs to enjoy the wilderness. They come complete with pristine, remote silence, where the crashing of the waves is the magnificent but solitary soundtrack to your holiday.

Much of the Outer Banks is just a sandbar, the Atlantic Ocean offering wild waves for surfing and jumping on one side. On the other side of the sand-banked islands, sometimes only a few metres wide in parts, a quiet and calm sound offers a glimpse back to the mainland USA and a fantastic water-lazing experience.

The beaches in places are long and wide, giving you plenty of space to yourself even in mid-August. The waters are, at different times, filled with all sorts of sea life, and you can regularly spot whales, dolphins and sharks. There have been thirty-four non-fatal shark attacks in North Carolina from 2006 to 2016, peaking in 2015 when there were eight. Conservationists warn that these are insignificant numbers and far more people die from bee stings than shark bites, but nonetheless it's a scary concept. Take a bow, please, the *Jaws* movie franchise, almost single-handedly responsible for giving sharks permanent bad PR.

Global warming is playing a part, as the water temperature becomes more favourable to these predators usually found elsewhere and to the fish lower down the food chain that they survive on. In December 2016 two great white sharks were tracked off the North Carolina coast. One was an adult called Manhattan and a few days later a pup was discovered and nicknamed Montauk, as she had first been spotted off the coast of Montauk in New York the previous August, described then as being relatively small

– measuring 4.6 feet (1.4 metres) long and weighing 50 pounds (22.67 kilogrammes). Then there's the adult great white shark called Hilton (named after Hilton Head in South Carolina) who is 12.5 feet (3.7 metres) long and weighs a massive 1,326 pounds (601 kilogrammes).[17]

Apart from the sharks (and there is a horn to warn people if one is spotted), it seems idyllic here to the casual holidaymaker. The further south you drive on this sandbank in the middle of the wild Atlantic Ocean, the more lost in isolation you become. Signs advising what to do should the island-wide hurricane alarm sound seem the only indication that sometimes life is not quite perfect here.

And then you pick up the local paper.

North Carolina is one of the poorest states in the US. Only eleven others have a greater percentage of their population living below the poverty line. The 'cheap' price of dinner and takeaway coffees and ice-creams compared to those in Washington DC or New York is only because of the locals' low income levels.

Unemployment, as a bald statistic, is not particularly worse in North Carolina than anywhere else in the US. In fact, if you rank the states in order of their unemployment rates, the Tar Heel State is seventeenth out of fifty. With an unemployment rate of 5.7 per cent, it is higher than the current national rate of 4.5 per cent but less than the worst state – West Virginia, at 6.7 per cent.[18]

However the absolute bottom of the pile, worse than all fifty states, is the special jurisdiction home to the nation's capital, the District of Columbia. Not a state but not a city either, the rate there is 6.9 per cent. But that would still be considered almost full employment in another westernised economy. It's an unemployment level that many other countries would gladly take. (The unemployment rate in Ireland is 6.2 per cent, down from 14.9 per cent at the depths of the financial crash; in Spain it's 18.6 per cent; in Brazil it's 13.2 per cent.)[19]

What is at times striking, right across America, is the level of poverty. Federal guidelines state that if your total household income for a family of four is below $24,250 (€22,625 as of July 2017), you are officially living in poverty. For a single person, that's a total annual household income of $11,770 (€10,983). According to the US Census Bureau's most recent report, between 2009 and 2012 more than one in three Americans (34.5 per cent) had at least one spell of poverty lasting two or more months.

It is common in big towns to see 'tent streets'. These are not makeshift affairs – they are long-term, nearly permanent structures. They consist of solid camping tents erected and tied to lampposts, fences or whatever other stable structure is nearby, and their edges weighted down by bricks and sandbags. Some have awnings or even deckchairs outside, along with shopping trollies filled with the life stories, the worldly possessions of the inhabitants of the tents. Rows and rows of them, usually on city highway underpasses – not dissimilar, but on a much smaller scale, to the shanty towns in parts of South Africa. But that is a country still emerging from apartheid: this is a country with one of the strongest economies on the planet.

In Washington DC, there is a tent row parallel to the city's most hipster street, near Union Station. And another tent encampment lies along the banks of the Potomac, right beside Georgetown University. On one particularly hot summer day, I was paddle-boarding on the water with friends and we spotted a woman up to her neck in the river. It is not a clean river so we started to paddle towards her, thinking she was in trouble and needed our help. As we neared her, she seemed a little distracted and we thought perhaps she was drunk and had fallen in. It was only when we got within 15 or 20 feet that we realised, almost too late, that she was washing herself. We spotted her tent on the bank and paddled away as quickly as possible, to afford her some tiny shred of dignity. Here in the capital city of the United States of America, in the area where the really wealthy live, about two miles from the White House, a woman was reduced to taking a bath in a river that is rated B- in the State of the Nation's Rivers index, where chemical contamination is such that intersex fish are regularly found there.

According to the national figures released in September 2016, almost one in seven people in the US live below the poverty line.[20] These numbers are declining. But in real terms that is 43.1 million men, women and children officially considered 'poor', living in one of the wealthiest countries on earth.

When you use a newer figure called the supplemental poverty measure, the situation is even starker. That measure takes into account deductions on the household income such as tax payments, work-related expenses and medical costs and factors in food-assistance programmes and housing subsidies.

While poverty rates are falling, they are still higher than before the financial crash of 2007. While Barack Obama and the Democratic Party campaigned about how they had turned around the US economy – which they did, and there are plenty of economic and employment indicators to prove that – not every household's lot has improved. Crucially, the numbers of those aged between eighteen and sixty-four who are in poverty is several percentage points higher than before the recession, before the Obama presidency. So during the 2016 campaign, the Democratic Party and Hillary Clinton argued how much better things were now, except more people are in poverty than were at the peak of the crash. They couldn't relate to her message. The recovery has never filtered down to them.

Furthermore, in the US nearly three out of five households remained in the same income bracket between 2009 and 2012. The whole tenet of the American Dream is to improve your life and improve the lot of your children. For most people in the US, this hasn't been happening recently.

This is what has fostered that sense of being 'worn down' by several years of struggling to make ends meet; of wanting a change; of being willing to try anything other than the 'same old, same old', which has not yet made a difference to their lives. It is the same feeling experienced by voters in the UK, in Ireland and across Europe who made their voices heard in recent elections too. In Ireland, voters turned away from traditional political parties, whom they don't view as having improved the economy sufficiently, taking a chance on independents who perhaps 'care' more. In the UK, we saw the Brexit result largely as a backlash, not just against immigration, but also reflecting a desire for a 'UK first' attitude, to take back control of the country. And in France, both major political parties were dissed by the electorate, who favoured a social-liberal and a right-wing populist party to contest a run-off, ultimately awarding the presidency to Emmanuel Macron.

————

In this vast nation, transportation is key. Not just to be able to get around on a personal level, but also for commerce. The car is king, but the train network – in places – is a lifeline and can be the preferred mode of transport for long distances for the less well off, as it's generally cheaper than flying and the same limits on luggage don't apply.

There's a train that runs from New York to Miami. The train that takes that twenty-six- to thirty-one-hour journey is called the *Carolinian*. One of its stops is in Rocky Mount, North Carolina. The train station is very quaint and cute. On the other side of the track is the old bus station, all wrought iron and red brick. It has been partially refurbished, as if waiting on a craft distiller or posh sandwich shop to open within. The town is well kept. No litter is visible anywhere, the lawns are perfectly manicured, as are the common green spaces, and any painted wooden facades are bright and freshly coated.

It truly looks picture perfect, like a movie set.

But when you look a little closer, some of those painted facades belie the ugly truth that many of them are vacant buildings. While they may be better taken care of here than in other parts of the US, the statistics give it away.

In North Carolina as a whole, roughly one in six people lives below the poverty line, according to the most recent figures available from the US Census Bureau (2015). That statistic is even higher if you're a child, female or non-white. It is also higher here than the US national average of 14.7 per cent. Things are improving in North Carolina, but 1.6 million people still live below the poverty line in a state where two of the country's top universities are located – Duke University and University of North Carolina in Chapel Hill. Annual student fees there are between fifty and sixty thousand dollars. A particular point of concern in North Carolina is child poverty. That is significantly worse here than the national average. Here almost one in four children lives below the poverty line .

It also has one of the highest rates of food insecurity. Families just don't have enough money to feed themselves. One in seven households receives food stamps here – again, the national average is one in eight. Of the 630,000 North Carolinians who receive food stamps (the new name is SNAP, the Supplemental Nutrition Assistance Program), nearly half are children and about one-fifth have a disability.

According to the University of North Carolina, 'poverty is this state's greatest challenge'. So much so that it founded the North Carolina Poverty Research Fund to 'explore, document and research the immense challenges of economic hardship in North Carolina'.

The North Carolina Justice Center takes up that point about the recovery tide not lifting all boats. 'The national economic recovery began in 2009, but it has yet to reach North Carolinians across the state.'

This may seem puzzling. If the rate of unemployment is so low as to be enviable to many European nations, why are so many so poor? The answer lies in the wages paid here and the horrible label of the 'working poor'.

North Carolina, the Tar Heel State, is the state that so celebrates industrial and entrepreneurial endeavour that its car registration plates bear the slogan 'First in Flight' in honour of the Wright Brothers, who flew their first plane in Kitty Hawk in the Outer Banks. But in this state, one-third of people are classified as the working poor. In other words, they are in employment, but the wages they receive are not enough to bring them above the poverty line. US economists define a 'poverty wage' as one where a full-time worker's income still places them below the federal poverty threshold to support a family of four. That is deemed to be $11.65 an hour. The national minimum wage is $7.25, and North Carolina is one of the states that pays only that, nothing more. (In Ireland the minimum wage is €9.25, around $10.) The North Carolina minimum wage has been at that level for eight years. That results in an annual paycheque of $15,080. The poverty threshold for a family of two is $16,020.

So in the USA, if you earn the minimum wage as set by the federal government, you are officially 'poor'. More than a third of the households that receive food stamps to make ends meet have a working adult in them. Only Arkansas has more people classified as working poor than North Carolina. Is it any wonder that people looked to someone as outwardly wealthy and successful as Donald Trump for help?

It is also a state of great income inequality. As a third of those working are struggling to make ends meet, in another part of the state, where those affluent and renowned universities are located, average wages are soaring. The US Labor Department shows private sector workers in the Durham-Chapel Hill area earn an average of $30 an hour. That's the highest hourly wage in the almost 200 city-metro areas that the department's study focuses on.

———

On that picturesque section of the Outer Banks, that fantastic stretch of beach, there are 544 registered school-age children. Even during the summer months when there is plentiful, albeit seasonal, employment in bars, restaurants, hotels and real-estate businesses, a local charity is still providing daily meals to 130 children, those one in four children whose families can't afford to feed them.

But Dare County, where those glorious Outer Banks lie, is Trump country.

Here and there, before the election, you would spot a yard sign or flag. Although Donald Trump's statewide margin of victory in North Carolina was 3.8 per cent, in Dare County it was a resounding 22.2 per cent, leaving Mitt Romney's 2012 victory margin of 16.2 per cent buried in the sand.

Again, ground down by uncertain, low-paying employment, by a situation that did not seem to be improving, voters were attracted to that same Trump talk about creating wealth and good-paying jobs.

But they also liked his conservative rhetoric. They liked the values and morals he spoke about, even if he does not necessarily live by them.

———

If you need carrots on Easter Sunday in Raleigh, North Carolina, you have a problem. Milk – well, you might be OK. But if you have some people suddenly stop by your house and you need to stretch the dinner, it's going to be an awkward situation. Not because there is a shortage of carrots in North Carolina – no, because none of the big grocery stores are open. Costco is closed. Publix is closed. Target is closed. Sam's Club is closed. Aldi is closed. And if you decide to go downtown for dinner instead, many of the restaurants are closed there too.

This is not the case in every state in the US – stores open or close depending on the culture of the state. But here in North Carolina, people are more religious than in the US as a whole, according to the most recent Pew Research Center Religious Landscape Study.[21]

Here more than three-quarters of adults identify as Christian – encompassing evangelical Protestants, mainline Protestants, historically black Protestants, Catholics, Mormons, Orthodox Christians and Jehovah's Witnesses. Around 20 per cent have no, or no particular, religion, 1 per cent are Jewish and less than 1 per cent identify as Muslim, Buddhist, Hindu or other world religions.

Compared with results on the whole for the US, there are more Christians and fewer members of the Jewish and Muslim communities. But there is a far higher percentage of evangelical Protestants and far fewer Catholics compared to the US overall.

Of those Christians in North Carolina, 75 per cent say God is 'very important' in their life, 21 per cent say God is 'somewhat important' and 77 per cent say they pray at least once daily.

When asked what their 'source of guidance on right and wrong' was, exactly half of the Christian population said they looked first to religion as their source of guidance. More than a third said they went with 'common sense', and the remainder opted for philosophy or reason or science. So most people turned to religion when they had a big decision to make, not common sense. That may explain why the issue of 'bathrooms' became so het up in North Carolina and then became an election issue across the nation.

The 'bathroom bill' – as North Carolina's House Bill Number 2 (HB2) came to be known – was one of the most contentious pieces of legislation to come into the statehouse building in recent years.

Wander the streets of Raleigh, North Carolina, or any of its cities and you'll see rainbow posters in the windows of shops, bars and restaurants bearing slogans like 'Y'all means ALL', 'We oppose HB2', 'HB2-bad for business'. One homeowner on the edge of the downtown area painted a mural on the side of their house that simply states 'all are welcome', alongside a large 'Raleigh, NC' in curly lettering with rainbow-flag colouring.

The bathroom bill passed through the North Carolina House and Senate and was signed into law by then governor Pat McCrory all within twenty-four hours on 23 March 2016. Its full name is the Public Facilities Privacy and Security Act. Its long name is 'An Act to Provide for Single-Sex Multiple Occupancy Bathroom and Changing Facilities in Schools and Public Agencies and to Create Statewide Consistency in Regulation of Employment and Public Accommodation'. A mouthful indeed.

The hysteria around the law, and the expediency demonstrated by lawmakers, might suggest some incident had happened to trigger this reaction. There is no known incident on record. In truth, it came about in reaction to a city by-law that Charlotte planned to pass, allowing students to use the bathroom of the gender that they identified with, rather than the one listed on their birth certificate.

This caused outrage among the conservative population; hence the pressure for a statewide law that would override Charlotte's ordinance or any similar one that any other NC city might wish to pass. While Charlotte is not the state capital – that's Raleigh – it is the largest city in North Carolina. It's a hub for this part of the country, second in size only to Jacksonville in Florida. Charlotte is the third-fastest-growing city in the United States. It's also the second-largest banking centre in the US, as two giants are headquartered there – Bank of America and Wells Fargo. A lump of gold found in this state by a twelve-year-old boy at the turn of the nineteenth century triggered the first American gold rush.

The bathroom bill basically specified that, in every bathroom or changing room in schools or public buildings, individuals could only use the facility that matches the gender on their birth certificate. And it went further. It prevented local councils from enacting local anti-discrimination laws. It rolled back previous ordinances councils had already passed to protect members of the LGBTQ community.

Supporters of this law claimed it would protect children against sexual predators who would seek to abuse the bathroom permission to assault vulnerable individuals. Opposers of the law retorted that sexual predators were unlikely to obey the rule of law about what bathroom they were supposed to use if crime was already on their mind.

But it passed, with detrimental effects on the state – it lost about $500 million and 1,400 new jobs.

Such was its impact that the National Collegiate Athletic Association (NCAA), which regulates the majority of sporting events for colleges and universities, pulled all of its sporting tournaments from the state for the 2016 and 2017 seasons. That alone cost North Carolina $250 million. The National Basketball Association (NBA) moved its 2017 All-Star Game – an event usually worth several dozens of millions to its chosen host city – out of the state.

Bruce Springsteen cancelled his concert there, saying, 'To my mind, it's an attempt by people who cannot stand the progress our country has made in recognizing the human rights of all of our citizens to overturn that progress. Some things are more important than a rock show, and this fight against prejudice and bigotry – which is happening as I write – is one of them. It is the strongest means I have for raising my voice in opposition to those who continue to push us backward instead of forward.'

Pearl Jam cancelled, posting a photograph of a handwritten statement online: 'The HB2 law that was recently passed is a despicable piece of legislation that encourages discrimination against an entire group of American citizens … We want America to be a place where no one can be turned away from a business because of who they love or fired from their job for who they are. We will be watching with hope and waiting in line for a time when we can return.'

Ringo Starr, Cirque du Soleil, Boston, the list of internationally acclaimed performers who refused to perform in North Carolina as long as the law was on the statute books goes on. Lionsgate moved the production of a new show from Charlotte to Canada; Broadway composer Stephen Schwartz said he would no longer allow his productions, which include the smash hit *Wizard of Oz*-inspired *Wicked*, to be performed there.

This law and the pushback it created made transgender rights and bathroom bills an election issue. Undoing such civil-rights gains mattered to the Democrats and to Hillary Clinton. Many Republicans and conservative voters, and Christians of both political persuasions, felt the law was correct. Trump voters felt he was more concerned with issues that mattered – like feeding their children, creating jobs and boosting the economy – than discussing bathroom privileges. Many voters in the poorer regions of Appalachia couldn't understand why so much energy was being spent on who went to which bathroom. As one red-baseball-cap-wearing man put it to me at a Trump rally, 'public restrooms aren't designed for hanging out in, so who cares which room you use, just get in, do your business and get out'.

So some voters flocked to Donald Trump because he wasn't clamouring for HB2 to be overturned, as Clinton was, but was focusing on 'more important issues'. Others moved to Team Trump precisely because he wasn't clamouring to have it overturned, assuming that meant he supported it. His true position as a candidate flipped. Initially he was against it, but then in July 2016, when he was the Republican Party's presumptive nominee, he changed his tune.

In an interview with the main North Carolina newspaper, the *News and Observer*, he said that he was 'going with the state' because they knew what was going on. That Trump opinion could be viewed as less about his views on civil rights for the LGBTQ community and more about speaking to one of the core tenets of Republicanism – keep interference in a state's business from Washington DC to a minimum.

The Obama administration weighed in, declaring HB2 breached federal anti-discrimination law, and issued an instruction that public schools were to let transgender students use the bathroom that matched their gender identity, threatening to withhold funding from those that didn't comply. When Donald Trump moved into the White House he revoked that.

As a side note, early in his administration Trump appointed the lawyer who defended the enforcement of HB2 by the University of North Carolina, John Gore, to be the assistant attorney general in the Justice Department's Civil Rights Division – a signifier of what was to come in the administration.

In March 2017, the North Carolina state government passed an amendment to HB2, called HB142, which repealed the original bathroom bill but did not return to the status quo that existed beforehand. Instead it attached a prohibition on local councils and agencies and so on from passing any local ordinances or by-laws to regulate access to bathrooms, showers or changing facilities. In other words, the Charlotte council that originally passed the law allowing transgender students to use whichever restroom they wanted cannot pass another similar law. At least not until 2020, when HB142 expires.

The confusing matter for those outside North Carolina was why this became an issue in the first place. In a state with a population of 9.9 million, there are just 38,000 transgender people. Drilling down further into the religious philosophy of the state, though, perhaps explains it.

With a higher than average proportion of evangelicals here, it's not a surprise to learn that nearly half of those who said they were a Christian of some form identified as Republican or leaning Republican, as opposed to 39 per cent who identified as Democrat or leaning Democrat. That is broadly in line with the nation as a whole, where 43 per cent of Christians fall into the GOP camp and 40 per cent into the Democratic one.

Those party lines work out when it comes to some core issues – for example, according to the Pew Research Foundation, on the issue of whether abortion should be legal or illegal, 44 per cent of Christians in North Carolina say it should be legal in all or most cases; 51 per cent say it should be illegal in all or most cases.

But on the issue of homosexuality (remarkably it's still a question on research surveys in the US), 46 per cent of North Carolina Christians say it should be 'accepted', but 42 per cent say it should be 'discouraged', while 11 per cent didn't have a particular opinion. That is out of step with the nation as a whole, where the majority of Christians say homosexuality should be accepted and just over a third say it should be discouraged.

On their thoughts about same-sex marriage, 52 per cent of Christians – remember, that's a majority of the population in North Carolina – said they opposed or strongly opposed same-sex marriage, 37 per cent said they favoured or strongly favoured it and 10 per cent didn't know or had no opinion. This, again, is less liberal than the nation as a whole, where 48 per cent oppose gay marriage and 44 per cent favour it.

It is worth pointing out that in June 2015 the US Supreme Court ruled in a 5–4 majority that the US constitution guarantees a right to same-sex marriage. Justice Anthony Kennedy authored the majority verdict then, and of the right of same-sex couples to marry, he said, 'no longer may this liberty be denied'. In an opinion described as having 'a style that is as pretentious as its content is egotistic' by one of the dissenting judges, the late Antonin

Scalia, Justice Kennedy wrote, 'No union is more profound than marriage, for it embodies the highest ideals of love, fidelity, devotion, sacrifice and family. In forming a marital union, two people become something greater than once they were.'

But according to the Pew Centre's research, more than half of the Christian populations in twenty-four states are opposed to gay marriage.

North Carolina has now been put on the map as a place where, in the twenty-first century, civil-rights inequalities were not only embraced but also, for a time, enshrined in law.

———

North Carolina was one of those 'watch states' on election night. How Donald Trump did in North Carolina would say a lot about how he would do overall. Both candidates peppered the state with appearances, including in the final week, when Clinton and her surrogates, including then President Barack Obama and Vice-President Joe Biden, made multiple visits. Trump and his team did the same, even doing two NC rallies on one day in the last week. On the final day of campaigning, Clinton made her last stop of the campaign in Raleigh, accompanied by Jon Bon Jovi and Lady Gaga. Trump also stopped in North Carolina that day, although his final rally of the campaign was in Grand Rapids, Michigan.

Many referred to North Carolina as the 'swingiest of the swing states'. Barack Obama won the state in 2008, but he lost it in 2012 to the Republican candidate, Mitt Romney. So with the sitting president already having lost, the warning signals were there for the Democrats that Hillary Clinton might not do so well, especially as she was so closely aligned with the Obama administration, which voters would ultimately hold against her.

What is notable about the 2016 turnout figures is that they were well up. Although Hillary Clinton lost, she got more votes than

Barack Obama did in both 2012 and 2008, and Donald Trump also got more votes than John McCain in 2008 and Mitt Romney in 2012.

There were more registered voters in the state, more actual votes cast than in any other year and percentage turnout was only slightly behind the modern record year of 2008 – when large numbers of African American voters helped Barack Obama carry the state. However, turnout of African Americans was significantly lower in 2016 compared with 2008 and 2012. It's frequently referenced that Barack Obama relied on that community to get him over the line here in 2008, and he had hoped they would do the same in 2012, as did the Clinton camp in 2016.

But the overall Republican turnout was way up in North Carolina in 2016, and that is ultimately what carried the state for Trump. There was a record turnout from Republican women – three out of four registered female Republican voters came out to vote in the 2016 election. Did they all vote for Trump? We don't know, but given the result, we can assume many of them did.

Democracy North Carolina analysed the data and the strongest turnout in the state was from Republican men and women and African American Democratic women. We can safely assume that those two groupings were voting for different candidates.

More than a third of independent or non-aligned voters didn't vote at all. Democracy North Carolina's research shows that more independent voters didn't vote than the number of Republican men who did vote. Half of those aged eighteen to twenty-five didn't cast a vote here either in the 2016 presidential election.

This all shows that neither candidate did much to inspire young people or independents. And that is only part of where it went wrong for the Democrats.

VISIT EARLY, VISIT OFTEN (OR HOW NOT TO LOSE A RACE BEFORE IT BEGINS)

F irm, creamy, yellow or sometimes a golden liquid. Capable of cheering up most people. Improves the taste of pretty much anything. Packed in gold-foil wrappers and smuggled across state lines into Wisconsin for decades. This 'contraband' trade began life in Ireland.

While not strictly a Class A drug, it might be treated that way by those on a strict diet. Since the 1950s, Kerrygold Irish butter has been banned in Wisconsin. The staple of many an Irish kitchen and dinner table is illegal in the state known as America's Dairyland.

Here, they take dairy products very seriously, and only items marked 'Grade A' can be sold. (The 1954 Wisconsin law had its origins in protectionism, as you might imagine.) So as Kerrygold butter is produced, tested and packaged in Ireland, and while it passes very rigorous grading there, it does not carry a Wisconsin or federal 'Grade A' marking.

And so for generations, in a state where around one in six people claim Irish heritage, trips were made to Illinois and Nebraska to 'bring back the butter'. One outraged woman who puts butter in her tea each morning (no, that's not a typo) told a local radio station that she travelled to Nebraska frequently. 'I'm hauling Kerrygold back in my suitcase and in coolers.' She told WTMJ News that she wanted to ask whoever was preventing her from getting the butter she wanted 'to stop it!'

Something of a blind eye had been turned to the ban for decades as, driven by market economics, the Irish butter was reasonably widely available. But some time after Donald Trump took office, and perhaps linked to his 'Buy American, Hire American' philosophy, the Irish butter ban began to be enforced again.

One conservative legal group, the Wisconsin Institute for Law and Liberty, even marked St Patrick's Day 2017 by launching a lawsuit against the Wisconsin State Department of Agriculture, Trade and Consumer Protection, responsible for enforcing the butter ban.

The penalty for violating the anti-Irish-butter law? A fine of $1,000 or more and up to six months in jail. A seriously salty business.

But where there's a will, there's a way. An enterprising business in search of the American Cream – sorry, American Dream, Old World Creamery of Sheboygan, announced in April 2017 that it had discovered a workaround to the problem of the banned butter. It was going to import butter in bulk from Ireland but process and package it on site, and then have it graded by the testers in Wisconsin, so it would have a 'Grade A' label. But it wouldn't be called Kerrygold any more: it would be Irishgold. But then Kerrygold launched a lawsuit against the Old World Creamery, saying Irishgold was too similar a name to its own, and as the butter was being sourced from a different Irish butter producer, it opposed the use of the name. In a speedy hearing, a Wisconsin court put a restraining order in place prohibiting the use of the Irishgold name. And so the range of butter legal actions just continued to spread.

While that case keeps churning, it does illustrate some things about Wisconsin. 1) The people like butter. 2) The notion of 'big government' making seemingly ridiculous regulations is not a fond one. 3) There is an entrepreneurial spirit. 4) There is 'people power'. And this is the key point to note.

For this story of 2016 and How the (Mid)West Was Won is not all about how Donald Trump won – part of it is about how Hillary Clinton lost. It has to be. He didn't win the popular vote, and he won a majority of electoral-college votes based on very slim victories in a number of key states. But a victory is a victory. As President Trump often says, if he thought he was supposed to win the popular vote as well he would have included that in his strategy. Instead he was very calculated, targeting states that were 'purple' in tone and with a strong message that would appeal to all. In a variation on Bill Clinton's 1992 campaign mantra (or rather that of his aide, James Carville), 'It's the economy, stupid', Trump just repeated, 'Jobs, jobs, jobs.'

When it's a two-horse race (and with no disrespect to the Green candidate Jill Stein or Libertarian Gary Johnson, the other significant candidates who competed for the White House, it is primarily a two-horse race), sometimes you get a lucky break. Could you argue that Wisconsin voters loved Donald Trump so wildly that they were wilfully voting for him regardless? Not quite. He won with just 0.7 per cent more of the vote – hardly decisive. But it was enough. Here in Wisconsin, the Badger State, the Dairy State, with a population of 5.78 million, 22,177 people gave Donald Trump a clear run at the White House. Flip this state to Clinton and he still wins. It's only ten electoral-college votes, but there was a similarly narrow margin in Michigan and a larger but still relatively slim one in Pennsylvania. So for Clinton, forever, it will be a case of what might have been. Had she mobilised and inspired a few more people, she probably would have got over that line, or in her words 'shattered that highest and hardest glass ceiling'.

As a side note, Jill Stein got 31,006 votes in Wisconsin, so Trump won by a lesser margin. If there was a PRSTV system, as we have in Ireland, who knows how the final tally would have ended up here if Jill Stein's votes had been redistributed. It's highly unlikely that many people who voted for a Green Party candidate would have given their (theoretically speaking) number two on a ballot paper to a climate-change denier.

And so our tale in Wisconsin is more of an allegory, a warning to all politicians, American or otherwise, of the perils that await you if you a) take your voters for granted, or b) ignore them entirely.

In Wisconsin, it's a tale of two halves, as it is for many states: urban liberal voters and rural conservative voters, swinging one way and then another, favouring Republicans in non-presidential years and Democrats in presidential cycles. Then it becomes a question of who can mobilise the greater turnout.

In Wisconsin, the media, and the campaigns to a certain extent, wrote off this state as 'blue-leaning' – likely to go for the Democrats. *Likely* but not definite, a key distinction that perhaps was overlooked in the decision by the Clinton campaign not to dispatch the woman herself to the state. Not even once.

However, as Professor of Political Sciences at the University of Wisconsin-Milwaukee Mordecai Lee points out, a campaign is not just one person. Tim Kaine, her running mate – America's dad, as he was affectionately known – visited America's Dairyland repeatedly; Bill Clinton made an appearance; the Wisconsin Democratic primary winner Bernie Sanders made an appearance. But that's all well and good. When the candidate doesn't come, it's not just about the rally. It can send an impression to the undecided voter that they're being taken for granted. And does any voter actually make a decision based on whether the candidate appears or not – who knows? It's true that most voters won't actually meet the candidate in person, but does *the knowledge* that the candidate at least was available actually matter? Perhaps not. But in a year when Hillary

Clinton was already suffering from an aura of entitlement and elite aloofness, when her main rival was wrapping her in the Washington malaise that he was pledging to cure, perhaps it wasn't a clever call. It makes the Trump strategy – a strategy everyone dismissed – look remarkably astute. Go there, go often. It doesn't matter if it's the same core group coming to each rally, driving for hours and queuing all day: it looks good. It says 'energy'.

As a couple of farmers in the north of the state put it, going to rallies is for 'city people' because 'they ain't got nothing else to do … when you farm, you farm seven days a week, you don't take time off of work to go to Washington DC to walk down the street'.

That statement reflects another part of Donald Trump's messaging that was borderline genius, if cartoonish in content: 'Drain the Swamp'. As the local legend goes (which has been debunked by urban historians) Washington, DC was built on a swamp, which leads it to have very humid summers. Donald Trump chose to equate a hot, sticky, unpleasant swamp with a capital city run by elites and out-of-touch professional politicians, who were all too cosy with lobbyists and the media. He gave the nomenclature of 'swamp dwellers' or 'swamp creatures' to this group of people that his target voters despised. A hatred he encouraged. As one must drain a swamp to clean it out, build on it and improve it, the same fate awaited Washington DC under his stewardship. He was going to 'drain the swamp'; rid it of its too-cosy inhabitants, clean it up and return it to the people in a functional state. As a marketing campaign, it is erudite, descriptive, active, evocative, sensory, memorable. It's simple. It worked.

First, those farmers view 'Washington DC' as totally disconnected from their lives. For them you have to actually work to make a living – work as in hard physical or manual labour. And second, referring to them as 'city people' and later 'fancy people': the average wage in DC is $25.13 per hour, and it's a majority black city – just 44.1 per cent of the population is white. Here in Wisconsin the average wage is $17.43 and 87 per cent of the population is white. While there may indeed be some 'fancy people' in DC, most are not. But it doesn't matter: the disconnect was already there, and 'Draining the Swamp' made it more real.

'Drain the Swamp' was also a perfect cry for Trump rallies. 'Drain The Swamp! Drain The Swamp!' the Trump fans would chant before moving onto 'Build the Wall! Build the Wall!' and then 'Lock her up! Lock her up!' with some 'U-S-A! U-S-A!' thrown in for good measure. Trump rallies always allowed for a real sense of community spirit – you could bond with those around you as you waited for hours in an aircraft hangar or cattle shed, leaving tired and hungry but exhilarated, as if having had some sort of evangelical experience. That is, of course, if you were a 'true believer'; if not, you often left the rally feeling dirty and disgusted.

Back in Milwaukee, Professor Lee too is sceptical of the import of rallies and appearances. He thinks that claiming Hillary Clinton lost the state because she didn't visit at any stage is 'the most ridiculous argument I've ever heard'.

Wisconsin has voted for the Democratic candidate in every presidential election since 1984. Ronald Reagan won that year. But his Vice President George H.W. Bush was not victorious in Wisconsin in 1988 when he sought the office of president. That year the state went for the Democratic candidate, Michael Dukakis – just one of ten states plus DC who did actually vote for him. On the face of it, it seems like George H.W. Bush won by a landslide in 1988 – 426 electoral votes to 111 for Dukakis. A hammering by anyone's standards, but not quite as stark if you factor in the popular vote – which, as we remind ourselves, does not matter in US politics – but Bush won 53.4 per cent of the popular vote compared to 45.6 per cent for Dukakis.

So after Wisconsin went for Dukakis, it followed in that blue vein in every presidential election cycle until 2016. Until Donald J. Trump.

But looking at those presidential election outcomes is not enough, says Professor Lee. It ignores the fact, he argues, that some of those elections were very close. He says that George W. Bush practically moved to Wisconsin during his two campaigns and still lost, but he lost by only a hair's breadth. Al Gore beat him by just 0.22 per cent in 2000, a mere 5,708 votes in a state with a population of 5.37 million at the time, and John Kerry beat him by 0.4 per cent in 2004. Professor Lee says that the fact that the Democrats won with Gore and Kerry was 'plain lucky, more than anything else. It wasn't because we're such a Democratic state.'

He also thinks the demographic make-up of Wisconsin favours Republican candidates, and that is why they end up, more often than not, with Republican governors. Those elections are in the opposite four-year cycle to the presidential elections and are not as sexy, so they generally get only the really committed voters – those who take their civic duty of voting seriously – who tend to be older, white, higher educated and middle class, and all of that in Wisconsin, a fairly conservative state, means they're Republican.

So when it comes to a presidential year, all those people are coming out to vote anyway, and the Democratic candidate has to do the 'heavy lifting' and encourage and motivate everyone else to get out, argues Lee. He makes this point so vehemently that, although he is entrenched in the view that Hillary Clinton's non-appearance did not cost her the victory here, it seems bizarre that, if much persuasion of Democratic voters is required, she didn't come here even once.

Sure, people may not bother to go to see a candidate at a rally, and in any event, you can only fit so many people in a room at once and you can only physically get to so many places. But it ignores the ripple effect of a candidate appearance. In American elections, much of the campaigning is done over the television. Door-to-door canvassing Irish style goes on, but not by the candidates. Getting into people's living rooms requires getting onto their TV sets. You can buy ads and in Wisconsin in the last week of the campaign in 2016 Donald Trump spent $52,042 and Clinton spent $25,542. But the real value is getting into the main evening news bulletins. Like in Ireland, and many European countries, voters of a certain demographic still sit down to watch the local affiliate main evening bulletin (in the US, TV is the top source of news for those aged fifty and over; those under fifty get their news online primarily, although one in four even of the youngest voters still watches television news). So television is where the candidate appearance is box office.

All politics are parochial and all voters – even on a subliminal level – must ultimately want to see the person who might be president in their state, to know they at least know where the place is and what it looks like. Seeing Donald Trump repeatedly in Wisconsin, in places like Green Bay and Eau Claire, got him a lot of free ad time. No matter how persuasive Bill Clinton, Bernie Sanders or any other surrogate is, they are the surrogate. They will never garner the air time on a news bulletin that the candidate will.

But as to Wisconsin being naturally conservative – it only removed its same-sex marriage ban in 2014, less than a year before the US Supreme Court ruled same-sex couples had a constitutional right to marriage, and even then the governor was still protesting it. Yet that conservative bent does not explain the sweeping victory that Barack Obama enjoyed – a 13.9 per cent margin in 2008 and a 6.7 per cent margin in 2012. Is it as the stock market ads warn – (voter) past performance is not a reliable indicator of future performance?

Professor Mordecai Lee thinks there's a reason for that too: 'racial solidarity'. As the potential first African American president, he stirred 'ethnic pride' in people. 'Which is understandable,' says Lee. 'I'm Jewish. If there were a Jewish candidate, every Jew in Wisconsin would vote, just out of ethnic pride. African Americans, out of ethnic pride, voted for Obama and just had a phenomenal turnout. It was a Noah's flood of African American voters who, on average, are not very consistent voters. The Obama thing is really the quirk of the statistics.'

But it's also a 'fluke' that Trump won, Lee ultimately concludes. And his chance of a second term here is not guaranteed.

The Wisconsin-based renowned Marquette Law School does a regular opinion poll. Two months into Trump's presidency they surveyed Wisconsinites and found that he had an approval level of only 41 per cent – that's a survey of the voters in a state that voted for Donald Trump. This is a state he won, and even they're not happy.

The big, famous universities are based in Milwaukee County, a deeply Democratic enclave, surrounded by the so-called wow counties of Waukesha, Ozaukee and Washington – so-called because they are Wow! So Republican!, surrounding the rock-solid blue Milwaukee. Even in 2016, 65.5 per cent of Milwaukeeans voted for Hillary.

But travel further up north and there's a different tale.

_____

Wisconsin is known as America's Dairyland. Its name comes from the native American word 'Meskonsing' from the Miami Indian tribe, which means 'river running through a red place', inspired by the state's red rock. One in ten Wisconsinites derive their income from the dairy sector or a job related to it. There are 10,000 dairy farmers in this state, in an industry worth $43 billion to the economy. Wisconsin produces one in every four pounds of cheese consumed in the US. Six hundred different varieties of cheese are made in the state.

The Green Bay area is just one of those more rural, farmland-filled regions of Wisconsin – historically competitive. Barack

Obama won it in 2008 but lost it – narrowly – in 2012, although he carried the state. While no poll across the Badger State showed Clinton behind at any stage, regional polls showed Trump leading 'big league' in this rural area.

And sure enough, at the Wisconsin Farm Show it's all about Trump.

Just as in Ireland and across the world, it's getting harder and harder to make a living from farming in Wisconsin. Duane is telling me all about it. He and his two brothers – all of them bachelors – bought a farm in 1992. They operate it themselves, and while they have thirty to forty cows at any time, they raise a lot of steers but they don't really make a profit. They sell milk too and some 'cash crops' – mostly soy at the moment. 'Everything's low now. Milk prices are low, steer price is low, crops are low.'

His friend Ray pipes in. The prices went down but the costs went up – hay and insurance have both rocketed. 'Fuel was high this past year or two as well,' he says, 'but at least that has come down.'

There's a particular problem in Wisconsin, though.

Ray fills me in on the 'corn craze'. 'A few years ago, there was $7 corn. It got to everybody's head. They filled their land with corn. They rented out land and were getting big bucks out of it because their corn was so high. Now all of a sudden they got five-year contracts, and the milk is half of the price that it was. And it's the same way with corn. But all the farmers are still stuck with that big high-priced rental property that they booked for five years. They got greedy.' But then the corn prices collapsed. The farmers had signed contracts for fixed rents on the fields assuming a certain yield from their crops. That didn't materialise. All sorts of farmers are feeling the pinch now.

There's what Ray calls 'farmers' welfare'. 'They [the federal government] used to give you a little bit, maybe $10 per cow or whatever. They kind of bailed you out. It helped a little bit but not enough to make it any different, but they had the name saying they tried to help the farmer out, you know? The last two or three years, we didn't get nothing.'

Duane is looking at some very large and shiny farm machinery, gleaming red against the blue sky and green surrounds of this airfield playing host to the 57th Wisconsin Farm Show. The scene is idyllic. But not the prices. 'That machine there would cost about half a million dollars.' There's just no way he could afford it.

'You'd probably milk for twenty years to pay for a thing like that with a small herd of cattle. Machinery has gone too high,' he says.

So what does he do if he needs a combine harvester? 'We borrow one or hire one. But them guys know that they're kind of scarce too, so for their machines ... they change the farmer a lot. About $10,000 a year you'd pay for them to fill your silo or your bunkers. You can't afford this machine but you can't afford to hire that guy that charges you too much.'

They really resent how immigrants were treated during the campaign. They say there's been a clampdown on illegal immigrant workers already in Wisconsin – or as Ray puts it, 'they kicked the Mexicans out of here'.

'The foreigners that they don't like here, they're the only ones that really like to milk and are really a good help, a reliable help.'

Duane doesn't have any immigrant workers on his farm because it's family run, but he said most in Wisconsin do, especially the big industrial farms. Many have up to 2,000 cows. They work three eight-hour milking shifts a day, so they can milk twenty-four hours.

Ray starts reminiscing about the strike in California a few years ago involving immigrant workers who were fruit picking. They refused to work because of the conditions and half of the crop died.

I heard similar stories about the immigrant workers in Kentucky as well. There, mostly Mexican farmhands and grooms are keeping the horse business going. They care for the work and they care for the animals. On several big farms the managers and jockeys are Irish and the grooms are Mexicans and no Americans are employed. But that is the origin tale of America – immigration.

At the farm show, although it's busy, the men are discussing the demise of the small farmer. Many smaller family farms have consolidated, as big industrial farms drive down the prices. Duane describes the sharp tale of his local vet. 'It's like he says, he used to drive a mile and he'd have a day's work. Now he has to drive a hundred miles just to get in a day's work. As a vet! Cause there just ain't the farms no more.'

Duane and Ray say they voted for Trump but they don't really care about who's in power, less so about Congress.

'Nobody seems to know about what happens out on the farm. They're thinking more or less of the stock market, they're thinking more about building bridges or building fences that keep other countries out and whatever. They don't really think about the farmer where the farmer's important. They raise the food for 'em and that's the last thing they think about,' says Ray. Both men sigh and look down at the dirt.

Elsewhere at the show, Dennis is seeking some shade from the late afternoon sun. He is more definitive. 'I voted for Trump,' he says proudly. 'It was the only option. I consider myself a Republican.' And he has no regrets so far because 'he is only doing what he said he was going to do. The other way [with a President Clinton], things could have really went south. Things could have really left the area. Big time.'

He started his own business in 2003 building barns and sheds. It all began when a friend asked him to build a horse shelter and she told her friends about it, and word of mouth spread and now, fourteen years later, he's still in business and has taken on two other men to help him. While the profits for farmers are down, he says he's having a great year and his sales are actually up. But he's from Mantua, home to 'Mantua Cranes'. Last year that company closed down, laying off 600 people. He thinks that will definitely have influenced some voters in a county that voted for Barack Obama twice and Donald Trump in 2016.

A potential customer for Dennis, small farmer Doug is making use of one of the deckchairs in the shed. He says quickly that he too voted for Trump: 'I figured I'd try to throw a monkey wrench in the freaking system and try to get this shit straightened out.' It's a common explanation from voters. It makes even more sense bearing in mind those unfavourability ratings – if as a voter you like neither candidate much, you might just lean towards the one who's more likely to shake things up a little. Exit polls on polling day ranked 'strong leader' as a popular reason for voters' selection – in hindsight, making perfect sense of the final outcome.

These men work long days and long weeks year round. They are not fans of those who don't, and anything looking like a welfare state is not something they're fans of.

Doug is the unofficial farm manager for his friend John, another bachelor farmer who needs a hand occasionally. John explains what irks him about the inequality he sees. He is a beef farmer but also has some crops that he uses himself – mostly corn – and some 'cash crops' that he grows just to sell. At the moment his cash crops are corn and soybeans. 'When I look at my cheque every year, this time of the year is perfect timing [it's approaching the end of the tax year when we're talking], and what I pay in for taxes and I see all these freeloaders. This time of year is when you really think about that.'

Doug pipes in with '60 per cent of the population are taking care of 40 per cent of the population in this country', alluding to the fact that, although the unemployment rate is lower than 5 per cent in the US, almost 40 per cent of people over the age of 16 – around 94 million Americans – are not working. According to the US Bureau of Labour Statistics, 94% of those in this cohort

– the so-called Not-in-Labor-Force – 'do not want a job now'[22]. The figure of 94 million is on the face of it a little misleading as it does include retirees, those with disabilities preventing them from working and full-time students, but it also includes those who chose not to pursue employment because many of the jobs available are so low-paying that they wouldn't be financially worthwhile when the knock-on costs of child-care and loss of benefits and welfare schemes are factored in.

Dennis agrees with Doug that there is too much heavy lifting being done by too few.

Again, Trump's strong, memorable message of leadership, economic growth, jobs, insulation and protectionism resonated with these farmers.

John says they had 'nothing to gain by having Hillary. It was a mess of a disaster.' He's not strictly a Republican but tends to steer towards them, he says, because the Democrats hit his paycheque harder – what's left of it.

'It was getting out of control,' says Doug. He's a small beef farmer too, living alone, and has been hit by a downturn in prices very badly. He bought his cattle herd three years ago and paid $250 a pound for them; this year he says they're only worth $25 a pound, and that's despite having fed them for three years. He sold them on at a loss but he had no choice, joking, 'that's the farm way. Buy high and sell low. So that way, you get a good tax deduction at the end of the year because you lost so much money.'

Despite the hard times, the men have a wicked sense of humour.

Putting a brave face on it, John jokes, 'I keep telling everybody, I wish I had a thousand head of cattle when they were at two-fifty a pound. Man, you know, I'd have been living in the Bahamas – not shovelling snow up here.' It's quite obvious he's only half-joking.

Doug is staying very quiet. His two acquaintances are registered Republicans. He doesn't want to divulge his allegiances. His friends give definitive answers when asked whether they voted for

Obama either time: 'Absolutely not'; and Dennis says he was really shocked that President Obama was even voted in for a second term. None of them voted for him in 2012, they say. But Doug laughs nervously when we're discussing the 2008 contest. I ask him politely but directly if he voted for Obama in 2008. And he says, 'Do you really want me to comment on that?' which I and the other men take to mean that he did. Some playful ribbing ensues. They're not holding this against him because he's pretty vehement in his dislike now of the forty-fourth president and his policies.

But more so, the three of them are sick of 'Washington' and the political class.

Dennis explains what frustrates him. 'In our system, to me, all this is back and forth, and back and forth between the parties'.

Doug continues his argument. 'They get mad at the Senate and the House of Representatives or whatever, they get … they bring in Republicans, they bring in Democrats, next time around we're not happy with them. It's back and forth.'

And like any good three-piece act, John finishes the point: 'Nothing gets done. Nothing happens.'

Doug can see that Trump is not a perfectly formed president yet, though. 'Sure, sure, he's got some bumps, he's gotta … You know, if he's gonna drain the swamp, there is a lot of draining to do.'

'I like that,' says Dennis.

The 'fresh new style' of Donald Trump, the non-politician, is attractive. It was attractive on the campaign trail. And here at this major farm show, several months into the Trump presidency, it's still attractive.

John expands. 'You look at what he's done and what he's up against. He's probably the best thing that we could have … somebody who's not a politician but a businessman. He might not be able to do it all but, by God, I think he's starting to swing … or let's put it this way, he'll slow it down from the devastation we were going in to.'

The other two nod in agreement.

They have no time, though, for those who are continuing to protest against Donald Trump.

'Come on,' says Dennis to no one in particular, 'this is our government. He was voted in and now we've got to work with him. That's how our government is set up. Majority rules.'

Except it's an unusual kind of 'majority rules' – it's a majority of electoral-college voters that rule, not a majority of the people. They shrug.

It's still curious. Just what did these Wisconsin men who spend their days, and often much of the night too, tending their land and their cattle see that made them believe that Donald Trump was one of them, that he better represented their interests than Hillary Clinton, a lifelong public servant versus a lifelong private money-maker?

But here's the theory from native Wisconsite Professor Mordecai Lee: 'In American politics, Republicans in our generation are brilliant tacticians compared to the lead-footed Democrats.' And some blame has to be laid at the feet of those managing Hillary Clinton's campaign. On 6 March Clinton lost the Michigan primary to Bernie Sanders. On 15 March, she just barely got over the line in the state of her birth, Illinois, beating Sanders by less than 2 per cent, and then on 5 April she lost the Wisconsin primary to Bernie Sanders. These were Democratic primaries and still she lost two out of three and just scraped the third to someone who had been an independent until just a few months prior. This should have been a loud warning signal to her campaign operatives. It should have screamed that populism was riding a wave, a wave that was in danger of dragging her under.

That populist force was not unique to either party. It is, after all, what swept Donald Trump to so many primary victories and to the prize of all prizes in November. But the Republicans, or at least those in the Trump circle, seemed to have cottoned on to this quicker and run with it. As Professor Lee says, they were the more 'brilliant tacticians'. This can also be seen in the case of a US Senate race here in Wisconsin in November 2016. In that instance, Senator Ryan Johnson was running against the former senator whose seat he had stolen six years previously. Johnson ran for re-election campaigning against Obamacare, the Affordable Care Act, as many Republicans did. The difference, though, is that Wisconsin had statewide laws before the Affordable Care Act was signed into law that meant around 90 per cent of Wisconsinites had health insurance all along. They were not a state that massively benefited. There were no millions of uninsured here brought into the net. Yet Senator Johnson managed to convince people who already had insurance through their employers that Obamacare was something they should feel threatened by. A genius argument. The presence or absence of the act would not dramatically impinge on their lives.

And so it is a case of 'It's the economy, stupid!' No matter where, what or how, if you're struggling, like many in Wisconsin are, you want to believe the person who tells you in a convincing way that they can make it better. If you're working hard and not rolling in disposable income, it can be easy to resent those who are not working hard and seem to be freeloading. And if you're tired and worn down from divisive politics, from politicians who don't understand *you* and *your* way of life, it's easy, and perhaps even logical, to take a chance on the known unknown candidate, rather than the known one.

WEALTHY AND RED IN MANHATTAN

An optician in his fifties, Sam Pirozzolo looked out the window to see giant flames in his front garden. It was 1 a.m. on a muggy August Sunday morning. Someone was ringing his doorbell to raise the alarm. The source of the fire was dangerously near his house. Firefighters would later tell him they smelled gasoline. It had been an arson attack. The blaze stretched more than 12 feet into the summer night sky. Sam would later say it looked like a burning cross from a Ku Klux Klan rally and that annoyed him even more. He hadn't set out to annoy anyone. It wasn't a racist symbol. It was a sculpture. It was made from foam insulation material and covered in latex paint, and therefore highly flammable. It was a giant capital 'T' with the stars and stripes of the American flag painted on it. T for Trump.

Sam had collaborated with local Staten Island artist Scott LoBaido on the pro-Trump symbol. Scott had designed and constructed the display. After it was set alight, the two men reported it to police as a hate crime and set about erecting a replacement. This one was even bigger – 16 feet tall. Scott describes himself as a 'pro-American, provocative artist for many years'. He describes the burning of his sculpture as 'an attack on my freedom of expression, on my freedom of speech'.

Sam was equally annoyed. Nobody claimed responsibility for the arson attack and in an angry Facebook post he blamed 'pro

Hillary Clinton thugs'. What made him feel better, though, was the phone call he received from Donald Trump himself, who wanted to make sure he was OK.

'After a while we put him on speaker phone. And he did this really cool thing, he told my kids their pops was a good guy.'

Staten Island can be described as a pocket of Trump in a hostile Democratic city. It was the only one of the five boroughs of New York City to vote for Donald Trump in the presidential election. In the Republican primary cycle he scored his biggest margin of victory in the whole country here on this small island.

Voters on Staten Island have long been regarded as a group where pollsters and political scientists could 'take the temperature' of the nation. Voters there replicate national averages in terms of home ownership, education levels and other demographic indicators. As in much of the country, there is a heroin- and opioid-addiction crisis too, which in turn has increased crime rates recently. They tend to lean Republican but, given they are part of New York City and the liberal social norms of the City That Never Sleeps, it is a middle-of-the-road swing county. There are actually more registered Democrats than Republicans on Staten Island, but they regularly cross party lines for presidential elections. Voters there, and across New York's five boroughs, also know Donald Trump better than any other voters in the country, so if Staten Islanders could effectively 'hold their noses' and vote for Trump anyway, that would be a good indicator of what would happen in swing counties in other states.

By contrast, it's hard to find too many people who will say out loud in Manhattan that they voted for Trump, but one in ten did – that compares with nearly six in ten on Staten Island. As in many other states, Hillary Clinton swept the populated urban areas, and Donald Trump won more individual but less populated rural counties, mostly upstate. He recorded huge victory margins in western New York, the area that is in the Appalachia region.

Trump actually did better overall in the state of New York than John
McCain did against Barack Obama in 2008. Then Obama won
with a margin of 28.1 percentage points; Clinton only managed a
margin of 22.5 percentage points in the state she calls her adopted
home and where she was a US senator from 2001 to 2009.

Staten Island is the third largest of the New York boroughs and
is known for its beaches, 170 parks and various summer-time,
beach-side tourist attractions. It's connected to Manhattan by
road-bridge and ferry. A cheap way of seeing the Statue of Liberty
is to ride the Staten Island ferry over and back.

The number of Irish names across Staten Island is remarkable
too. It *is* New York so there is no shortage of Irish bars either. The
railroad travels the length of the island. Stop at the Great Kills
station and find Flanagan's Tavern, stop at Eltingville station and
the hotspot is Joyce's Tavern.

But it's not just Irish bars that are numerous – in the run up
to the election it was the Trump–Pence garden signs that caught the
eye: pieces of laminated cardboard on sticks that were hard to find
elsewhere in New York City or, indeed, a giant foam capital letter T.

But Staten Island is home to a majority of white blue-collar
workers, exactly like those who formed the bedrock of Trump's
support in those key states up through the spine of the Appalachian
Mountains. It is the traditional residence for members of the New
York police and fire departments. The joke on Staten Island is that
if you live here and you're not a cop, then you're related to one.

Locals here say they're used to people shooting their mouths
off, but sometimes Trump goes too far. They all voted for him but
would be happier if he operated a bit of 'radio silence' for a while.

Joseph Borelli was born and raised on Staten Island. He's a
council man and represents the people of this borough on New
York City Council, located in Manhattan. He lives in Annadale
now, with his wife and baby son. Annadale, on the island's south
shore, has typically larger and more expensive homes than much

of the rest of the island. There's a waterfront area that spans 18 acres known as 'Spanish Camp', as it was originally founded as a summer colony by the Spanish Naturopath Society in the 1920s. It's also an area that suffered quite serious damage during Hurricane Sandy in 2012.

In addition to his council position, Joe teaches political science at the College of Staten Island. He describes himself as 'a Trump guy', and in a city that is overwhelmingly Democratic, he popped his head up to be the co-chair of Trump's New York campaign team.

Trump's support for law enforcement played well with residents here of every persuasion. He was popular, too, with the more conservative, older white Catholic voters who express annoyance that the federal government is coming for their guns and their tax dollars while giving the appearance of doing nothing about possible terrorist threats and radical terrorism.

Healthcare and access to benefits are big issues too. Many of the residents are police or firefighters who were at Ground Zero on 9/11 and now have chronic ailments caused by the toxic fumes they inhaled. They've had difficulty getting access to medical benefits and have even had to resort to a march on Washington to try to raise awareness. Donald Trump hits a lot of those hot-button issues for them.

Joe says he didn't have to think long before deciding to vote for Trump. He backed him before the primary season, when he had sixteen other Republican candidates to choose from, and he certainly backed him in the general election.

'I'm full force behind him. He's the hometown guy. We live in a city where we get dictated to by liberals and progressives, and a lot of people in the Republican Party are very frustrated by that. Here on Staten Island, as people who appreciate loud and bombastic tones – as New Yorkers – it's no surprise we get attracted to someone like Donald Trump.'

But as New Yorkers, some of what the now President Trump says is even a little much for the brash Staten Islanders.

'He's someone who was never in politics before and, yes, he says things that are at times cringeworthy. A lot of Americans can differentiate between some of his rhetoric, some of his controversial things that he's said, and his actual policy. I think you're seeing a large segment of the American population actually agreeing with him and saying, yes, we don't want a porous southern border.'

Joe likes that Trump challenges the status quo, that he didn't just aim for the 'same old, same old' policies of his predecessors.

'People don't like Donald Trump out there – there are people who don't support him and that's part of the American system. We have an extremely diverse electorate and an extremely vocal population who are going to voice opinions whether others disagree or not.'

Although he's a New York City councillor, Joe says he feels like a minority in New York City, and that is frustrating for him and it's frustrating for other conservatives in other parts of the country living in Democratic strongholds. They feel, he says, like they have to suppress their true opinions and their true beliefs. But not anymore.

'I live in this city and we almost get dictated to by the Democratic Party, both at state and city level. So having someone who not only has a centre-right message but someone who's not afraid and doesn't come with the same guilt that you often see Republicans facing, that to me is refreshing. I want someone who's going to be unapologetically right-leaning.'

He and his constituents want to see Washington DC shaken up as well and are putting their faith in Trump. Republicans and Democrats here feel very bitter about how long it took the House and Senate to vote to extend the Zadroga 9/11 Health and Compensation Act. That piece of law provides healthcare coverage to the first responders who worked so tirelessly after the September eleventh attacks and who are now suffering from Ground Zero-related afflictions.

The law is named after James Zadroga, a thirty-four-year-old detective who died in January 2006 from health complications caused by the length of time he spent in lower Manhattan inhaling the toxic air in the wake of the World Trade Center attack. He spent some 500 hours going through the debris of the Twin Towers searching for survivors.

Around 200 New York City police officers and firefighters have died from 9/11 related illnesses; another 33,000 first responders and survivors suffer from a range of ailments all these years later, including fifty different types of cancer that are linked to the toxins released that day.

In 2015 the law was passed, extending benefits for seventy-five years, which should take account of the lifespan of everyone who responded on the day of the 2001 terrorist attacks. However, it literally took years to get through Congress and Joe Borelli says the people there have long memories and will not forgive senators and congresspeople who did not vote for it. He believes that under President Trump such worthy legislation would not have taken so long.

That perceived ability to get things done is what makes Donald Trump attractive to businesspeople too.

––––

Jason Meister describes himself as a real-estate entrepreneur, investment sales broker and luxury-home entrepreneur – titles, perhaps, that Donald Trump would have ascribed to himself at one stage of his career.

Jason was involved with the Trump campaign at a grassroots level in Manhattan and attended the Republican National Convention. He has written many opinion pieces promoting

Trump and now regularly appears on Fox News and Fox Business to parse President Trump's actions. He is convinced that Trump is the best man for the job. In one article, he described the business acumen that he felt Donald Trump would bring: 'Deal-making in this town is known to be cutthroat and unforgiving. I can tell you from personal experience that it's not for the faint of heart. Trump knows first hand about clawing your way back when the chips are down.'

Jason's father, Stephen, is one of the best-known real-estate litigation attorneys in New York City. He was Trump's lawyer for many years until 2013, so there is a family connection in their support for Trump. Stephen Meister has written a book on the 'real estate revolution', which, when published in 2011, Donald Trump described as 'an insightful and comprehensive book that explains what happened during the financial crisis and offers possible solutions to what we're facing now'. Meister Senior represented Trump in 2013 when the now president took an ethics case against New York Attorney General Eric Schneiderman, who was then investigating Trump University for fraud. The ethics case was ultimately dropped, and after his inauguration President Trump settled the Trump University class actions and fraud case for a total of $25 million, without admission of liability.

Jason and I meet for the first time in a corner office of a shining corporate building near New York's Grand Central Station. The wall-to-wall windows give a fantastic view of Manhattan and look right across at Donald Trump's first major building project in the city – the Grand Hyatt hotel on the corner of Lexington Avenue and 42nd Street. The background to that deal is well catalogued in Donald Trump's book *The Art of the Deal*, and while he took a gamble and leveraged himself in a complicated fashion, he can be credited with helping to rejuvenate a section of New York that had been a firm no-go area for some time.

Jason wouldn't look out of place in a Trump family photo: young, put together, sharp suit, styled hair, confident air. He could not be more dissimilar to many of the people I met in the heart of Appalachia, yet his thoughts on Donald Trump are almost identical. His reasons for supporting him are the same.

He is effusive in his praise of Trump. 'He's a world-class negotiator. He's really in a lot of ways a messenger from the American people that they're fed up with Washington DC, and it's on both sides of the aisle. It's Democrats and it's Republicans, I think; you've come off eight years of President Obama, and we've had enough. We want change and Trump represents change. He's incorruptible. Finally we have a businessman which Washington DC has lacked and so that's to me what's really going on.'

As a businessman himself, working in what he describes as the 'shrewd business of New York real estate', Jason says he and his counterparts want to see a pro-business CEO of the United States, one who understands industry and the dangers of over-regulation.

'I think we need to unleash the economy. Republicans, Democrats, they're career politicians. They don't understand business. They don't understand tax policy. This is a very successful businessman. He's run an incredible company. He took a mostly outer-borough residential portfolio and turned it into a major trophy office-tower portfolio, which includes Trump Tower and other landmark buildings. He renovated the Wollman ice-skating rink. He's done incredible things for this city, he's done incredible things for this country so, you know, when you take away the rhetoric – and I know he's said some controversial things this election – you see a man who's done a lot and has a lot of skills to offer this country and I think it's time for the American people to get behind him.'

Jason and his family are wealthy Republicans, the ones who maybe focus more on the right-leaning capitalist policies of the Republican Party and are less concerned with, or aligned to, conservative social values. With all the regulations and controls that were introduced to control financial markets and industry, Jason describes the eight years of the Obama administration as 'abysmal'.

'I really wanted change, and I wanted to see a candidate who …' He searches for the right words. 'Washington DC has lacked business acumen and he's the only candidate that offered that. When you compare him to Mitt Romney [the Republican party nominee in 2012], Mitt was a businessman but he wasn't … well … he was more of a country-club Republican. Donald Trump is a New Yorker. He's a doer. He gets things done. He will get things done. He's also a unifier – he cut his teeth on New York City real estate – it's not easy to get two people together to make deals, to crack down on the unions. He had to deal with the unions when he built buildings. He knows how to get things done.'

That sense of 'getting things done' and cracking down on the unions are precisely the reasons so many people in New York City, in particular in Manhattan, *didn't* vote for him. There are long lists of well-documented cases of business partners, residents, contractors and others who feel he wasn't a great person to work with or for, but in certain circles he's considered a tough but respected businessman.

Talking about America under President Trump, Jason says he's 'excited'.

He sums up succinctly the attraction that Donald John Trump, son of Queens, has for New York elites as well as the blue-collar workers across the US.

'He paints bold colours and he speaks very brashly, but when you strip it away from the rhetoric, he's saying what the American people say around their dinner tables. He's not afraid to say those things and that's what he's tapped into – a geyser of frustration in Americans – and it's such a relief and it's such a breath of fresh air to finally say what all of these Americans have been thinking.'

His words remind me of what some very glamourous ladies at the Republican National Convention in Cleveland, Ohio in July

2016 said one day. 'Donald Trump is just so refreshing. He makes it OK. All those beliefs that you have buried in your back yard, all those thoughts that you have tucked under your mattress, he makes it OK to bring those out into the light and say them out loud.'

He tapped into pent-up frustrations. He identified something in every man and every woman, something they recognised in him. And they came out to vote for him – because of what he said and in spite of what he said.

Conclusion
IT'S A NUMBERS GAME

There had been much talk about the 2016 election season being 'a bit dull'. It was set up to be Bush versus Clinton. Again. Who would possibly be interested in a dynasty showdown? Both former Florida Governor Jeb Bush and former Secretary of State, US Senator for New York and First Lady Hillary Clinton had been engaged in extensive fund-raising and had a lot of big-money backers well in advance of declaring their candidacies. The general consensus was that the 2016 cycle would be difficult to endure. Who would be invigorated by that match-up: two safe career politicians? Seasoned US political commentators said all throughout late 2014 and early 2015 that it would be difficult to get, and keep, the electorate engaged in 2016. Nobody would be interested; nobody would care. Famous last words.

Just four weeks into the primary season Jeb Bush announced he was 'suspending his campaign', bowing out of the race. ('I'm suspending my campaign' is political speak for 'I'm quitting but should something disastrous happen to the frontrunner and I look like I might be in with a shot after all, I reserve the right to get back in the race.') After just three contests – Iowa, New Hampshire and South Carolina – he'd been outmanoeuvred by the arch-negotiator and deal-maker himself, Donald Trump.

As winter turned into spring turned into summer and state after state was traversed, contender after contender fell by the wayside. Trump looked set on an unstoppable path to the Republican

Party nomination. On 4 May the Ohio governor, John Kasich, the last man standing against Trump, bowed out of the Republican primary race, and it was all over bar the formalities for the New York billionaire businessman.

Throughout the campaign and up until polling day, John Kasich remained one of the few senior members of the Republican Party not to endorse Trump. He didn't vote for him either. His spokesman confirmed that he simply could not bring himself to vote for Trump and would never vote for a Democrat so instead he wrote the name of the 2008 Republican nominee, John McCain, on top of his ballot paper.

Donald Trump delivered a masterclass in disruption. Credit where credit is due. Young people are becoming billionaires in Silicon Valley in California for their ability to 'disrupt' traditional industries and reap huge rewards, score giant successes and make a lot of money. That is exactly the model Donald Trump used in the 2016 election cycle. You can question whether he viewed it like that, whether he set out to do it or who actually deserves the credit. And of course there's the belief shared by the four main US intelligence agencies that Russia interfered in the process – not by stuffing ballot boxes but by cyber-disruption: email hacking, 'fake news' bots and orchestrated anti-Clinton social media campaigns.[23] The now President Trump is sensitive about his victory, decisive as it was, because so many people question the legitimacy of it and point out that a minority of American people actually voted for him. President Trump himself has alleged that millions of illegal immigrants voted for Hillary Clinton and that cost him the popular vote. He even set up the Presidential Advisory Commission on Election Integrity to investigate.

We have not yet heard from Trump about the strategic planning behind the mastery of his campaign. Perhaps one day we will; perhaps we won't. But for now, we'll give him the benefit of the doubt for that disruption and for getting a little lucky with the confluence of events that was happening in American life and in the American media.

Given how the Founding Fathers framed the electoral-college system, and how so many states are resolutely and staunchly for one or the other party, any candidate who makes it through the primary system and becomes the official nominee is almost guaranteed a certain number of votes, based on the states that always vote exclusively Democratic or exclusively Republican and never ever waver. In the case of the Democrats, that's a solid 222; in the case of the Republicans, that's a solid 163; and it was no different in 2016.

The balance of power, as always, lay with the voters in the swing states. And this is arguably the unfair part of the system. Trump repeatedly referred to the system as 'rigged', and perhaps in some ways it is. All voters' votes do not carry the same weight across the US. All votes are not equal. In 2016, and perhaps this is the start of a new pattern, the voters in lower-populated states and swing states had, and perhaps now will continue to have, a greater say in the outcome of presidential elections.

The inequality between voters in different states is clearly evidenced if we look at the case of the most densely populated state, California, and the least densely populated, Wyoming. All states get two electoral-college votes for their two senators. The votes that make up the balance are allocated in accordance with the number of members of the House of Representatives. They are broadly allocated based on population in a state but not equally so. In California – a resolutely Democratic state – there is only one electoral-college vote for around every 670,000 voters. In the state of Wyoming – a Republican stronghold – it works out at one electoral-college vote per 186,000 people. So therefore the people of Wyoming have more value than the people of California.

The situation is even more unequal when it comes to swing states, especially as, unlike many primary contests, in the general election electoral-college votes are not awarded proportionately. With two exceptions, if you win even by a margin of one or two votes, you win all of the electoral-college votes available. So while the people of Wyoming may have more value than the people of California, neither have as much power as the voters in somewhere like Pennsylvania who can make or break a president.

In 2016, this was particularly stark because a mere 77,745 people spread across the states of Michigan, Wisconsin and Pennsylvania were all that stood between Donald Trump and Hillary Clinton and who won the White House. That cohort of people is the cumulative difference between the number of votes the two candidates in those three states received.

Donald Trump finished with 304 votes: a candidate needs 270 to win.[24] Barack Obama had won all three states in 2008 and 2012 and so it was assumed that Hillary Clinton would do the same. But those 77,745 voters in Michigan, Wisconsin and Pennsylvania handed Trump a total of forty-six electoral-college votes, which took him over that magic 270 threshold and on into the White House – despite the fact that across the fifty United States and the District of Columbia 2,864,974 more people voted for Hillary Clinton than Donald Trump. But that is the system the Founding Fathers put in place.

The opposite of disruption in this political context is legacy. In 2014 and the first half of 2015 we were expecting a legacy election – Jeb Bush versus Hillary Clinton. First we saw disruption in the Republican primary process. Donald Trump repeatedly got on stage with multiple party colleagues and owned the conversation. When not doing those debates, he owned the news agenda. He made his rallies compulsive viewing so the TV networks covered them live – a rare occurrence. Even when he became the party's official nominee, he continued his campaign of disruption, whereas Hillary Clinton continued to run her campaign in a 'legacy' or traditional style.

Going on the basis of the previous six elections, Hillary Clinton was expecting to have an easy 242 electoral-college votes in the bag come Election Night, based on Democratic stronghold states and Democratic-leaning states. The poorest Democratic performance since 1992 was that of John Kerry in 2004, who finished with 257 electoral-college votes. Hillary Clinton did even worse. She finished with 227.[25] Had she managed to persuade those extra 77,745 voters in those three states, she would have finished with 273 electoral-college votes and the keys to the White House.

We also can't ignore that part of the disruptive campaign Trump ran was designed to circumnavigate the traditional media, and not only that, but also to make the mainstream media out to be tyrants. By devaluing what established commentators said, he inoculated himself and his voters against the impact of the distasteful, offensive, foot-in-mouth errors. Anything negative he said was digested as 'well, that's just the spin the mainstream media is putting on it'. Trump did this so successfully that, by the time the *Access Hollywood* tapes came out, his voters who may have been initially stunned by them managed to correct themselves and stay on the Trump Train.

There is a whole other thesis in the role that the US media played in this election and how voters sought out news from self-confirming sources. If you're a conservative, you watch Fox News to have your world view reaffirmed. If you're a liberal you read the *New York Times* or watch MSNBC for the same reason. If you're a younger person, you get your news almost exclusively online, in a sphere that is practically unpoliceable. US broadcast journalists are not bound by the code of conduct that requires them to be impartial, as journalists working for public-service broadcasters in Western Europe are. They are not funded by a mandatory licence fee, but rather by commercial revenue streams, so the rules of engagement are not comparable. Viewing figures are the driver of coverage – in both tone and content.

Donald Trump figured out early on that many in the media, many established political commentators, like to criticise rather than praise. To provide a check on power, a key job of journalists involves fact-checking and presenting to viewers, readers and listeners the flaws in an argument so those voters can make their own deductions and vote accordingly. As the legendary journalist Carl Bernstein, who helped uncover the Watergate scandal, puts it, a journalist's job is to provide 'the closest and best attainable version of the truth'. Donald Trump, the reality-TV mega-star, was clever enough to realise that scandal, chaos and controversy make much better television than responsible, policy-driven rhetoric. He billed himself as rogue and exciting, and Hillary Clinton looked boring. He drove away his primary contenders by giving them unflattering but sticky monikers – 'low energy Jeb', 'little Marco' and 'lying Ted', and then in the general election it became 'crooked Hillary'.

Just as Franklin Delano Roosevelt transformed campaigning through the use of radio, and John Fitzgerald Kennedy did so through television, Donald John Trump did it through Twitter. That became his direct communication method to his supporters and the wider public. It went straight into people's hands and pockets: they did not have to do anything to tune in – no making time to sit down and turn on the radio or television or buying a newspaper. His message was not filtered or put into context by the media. There was no limit to how often he could contact his audience, no requirement to include anyone else in the conversation.

But Trump's honed ability to manipulate the media, and the smart decision to target states where voters had a disproportionate influence on the outcome, only worked because so many of those voters were ready to receive his message.

As a very late supporter of Donald Trump, Speaker of the House of Representatives and Republican Wisconsin Congressman Paul Ryan put it the morning after Trump's victory: 'Let me just say, this is the most incredible political feat I have seen in my lifetime. This is something you've heard me say time and again. Seven out of ten Americans, they do not like the direction our country is going. Many of our fellow citizens feel alienated and have lost faith in our core institutions. They don't feel heard and they don't feel represented by those in office. But Donald Trump heard a voice out in this country that no one else heard. He connected with – he connected in ways with people no one else did. He turned politics on its head.'

That 'voice' that Donald Trump 'heard' was largely the voice of older, angry, white, less well off, less well educated voters, teetering on the edge of the middle class. In particular, he targeted those individuals in the largely swing states in the Appalachian region. These were the people whose value system taught them that working hard and being straight and honest would give them a fair shot at life, that the American Dream was attainable. These were the people for whom the American Dream seemed to be getting further and further out of reach.

That concept can be sneered at, but it strikes at the core of large numbers of people in this country. It speaks of hope: it is the same concept that Barack Obama ran on so successfully in 2008 and 2012.

The American Dream is described as 'a deal' by John Zogby, a political analytics and polling expert: 'I make a deal with this country. I work hard, I put food on the table, I pay my bills, I get my children to college, and then they do better than I'm doing. And the growing sense that, number one, I'm not doing as well as I should be doing – other people are doing much, much better and I'm losing ground financially – and then what about my children? Regardless of the reality, it's the perception. I send my children to college. That's part of the deal, and then they graduate, especially after the recession, and I don't know what happens to them. And the sense now is that this is the first generation of children who are perceived as doing worse than their parents.'

Or as one young writer put it in an unpublished college manuscript decades ago, Americans have a 'continuing normative commitment to the ideals of individual freedom and mobility. The depth of this commitment may be summarily dismissed as the unfounded optimism of the average American – I may not be Donald Trump now, but just you wait; if I don't make it, my children will.'[26]

Who was the author of that commentary on the permanent sustainability of and quest for the American Dream? One Mr Barack Hussein Obama.

———

Almost three out of every five American households are in the same income bracket as they were in 2008. That's nearly a decade without financial improvements. A sense of failing causes a feeling of anger, not just a financially driven anger but also a cultural and demographic anger, a thought process along the lines of 'I'm not doing as well as I had hoped to do, but not only that, others are doing better than I am.' And by those 'others', they often mean newcomers.

There are more immigrants living in the US than in any other country on earth. About forty million people living in the US were born in another country. As of 2015 it was home to about a fifth of the world's migrants.

But on the issue of deporting immigrants – something that Donald Trump made much capital from on the campaign trail – there is also a question about the messaging on the Democratic side. During the Obama administration, from 2009 to 2016, around three million people were deported – a considerable amount more than the two million immigrants deported by his predecessor George W. Bush between 2001 and 2008. More immigrants were deported by Obama than by any other president.

Yet Donald Trump's campaign team were able to effectively paint the forty-fourth president, and the wider Democratic Party, as 'soft' on immigration. That belief was further underlined by Hillary Clinton's decision to spend a reasonable amount of time effectively courting the Latino vote. Those two positions should not have been mutually exclusive. It is possible for a party, for a president, to want to offer a legal pathway to citizenship and to a better life while still actively enforcing the law of the land. That was exactly what Barack Obama said he was doing – he just did not do a good job of explaining that to people. He too was deporting criminals, the people Donald Trump described as 'bad hombres'. Though less than half of the 333,000 immigrants deported during 2015 – the most recent year statistics are available for – had criminal convictions. That means most of those were law abiding but were deported anyway – hardly a 'soft on immigration' position. However, nobody that I met who declared as a Trump supporter or attended a Trump rally ever had anything to say other than 'Obama is soft on immigration'.

However, while we see Donald Trump's anti-immigrant rhetoric resonating in some states, we don't see it to the same proportion in states that actually are home to most immigrants. California is home to 25 per cent of the immigrants in the US and New York is home to 10 per cent – both gave Hillary Clinton decisive victories. Texas is home to 11 per cent, and although Trump won there, he did not win a majority of the counties actually along the border with Mexico – those voters who live alongside immigrants day in and day out. In other states, though, it is that fear of the Other that allowed Trump's rhetoric to take hold.

A point that cannot be ignored is that, no matter how appealing Donald Trump was, how he disrupted political campaigning, Hillary Clinton was a poor candidate. Her campaign had faults – many of which are discussed in detail elsewhere and don't need to be repeated here – but the fact remains that she was a candidate that not even many Democrats were passionate about. I know several individuals who are devout Democrats, who have given up holidays and family time since they were teenagers to canvass and participate in phone banks and fundraise for all sorts of candidates, who worked for several years in various forms for the Obama administration and who did not vote for anyone in the 2016 presidential election. They cared too much about their civic responsibility to boycott the ballot paper entirely, but they left the section to select a presidential candidate blank, voting only in the lower races.

With political experience comes political baggage. However, as one Democrat who had been a quite senior administration official during the early Obama years said, 'I wasn't able to hold my nose and vote for her anyway. But the Republicans are made of steelier stuff and more of them were able to hold their noses and vote for him anyway.'

The biggest outstanding question of them all, of course, is can Donald Trump do it again? Can he win the hearts and minds of the people of Appalachia and beyond again? It's too early to judge at this stage – even his supporters say that. While he has made moves to follow through on campaign promises that have already been well received, he has also made some potentially damaging plans. For example, in Trump's first budget, in a bid to cut costs so that he can ultimately cut tax rates, he proposed closing a lot of regional commissions. What's on that list? The Appalachian Regional Commission (ARC) and other regional commissions, the US Economic Development Administration and the US Department of Housing and Urban Development's Community Development Block Grant programme, as well as other programmes impacting this region. According to its own figures, ARC has invested $75.5 million specifically to diversify the economy in 236 coal-impacted counties across nine Appalachian states. It claimed in March 2017 that that money was projected to create 6,800 jobs, benefit more than 23,000 students and workers and attract linked investment and spending totalling $142 million into the economy of the general region. Of that $75.5 million that it had invested as of March 2017, it had only been able to fund one in four of the projects in the thirteen-state grouping that had requested assistance. ARC says it received applications looking for a total of $280 million. If it closed down, what would happen to the people it is charged with helping?

But notwithstanding the rollercoaster ride since Donald Trump's election win, those who voted for him are happy with how he is doing and are mostly not fazed by the scandals reported since he took office. He has low satisfaction-poll ratings as president, but he had low ratings as a candidate. He is a polarising individual. If you loved Trump before the election, you're likely to still love President Trump. If you hated Trump before the election, you're likely to still hate President Trump.

Take Chris Vitale in Michigan, the third-generation auto worker and union official living in a Democratic area in one of the three states that handed the victory to Trump. Fundamentally, Chris rejects any sort of 'Russia connection' with Donald Trump or his campaign team and believes many of the stories appearing in the newspapers, from 'leaks' and 'unnamed sources', are creations by a hysterical anti-Trump mainstream media. 'I guess to me, it's sort of a non-issue,' he told me several months into Trump's presidency. 'I think it's a bunch of smoke and mirrors to distract from the idea that Hillary Clinton was a horrible candidate. She lost on her own merits. They don't want to accept that, so we have to create some narrative for why she failed. I think that's really what this is. People forget too, and it's probably not as nuanced in Europe, that in these same elections where Donald Trump was elected president, there were many other smaller seats, governorships, senators, congresspeople, and the Republicans won in a landslide. Did the Russians influence that, too?'

The Republican Women of Powhatan County in Virginia are equally happy with his performance. Months after the election, chairwoman Jean Gannon told me she still fondly remembered the night of Donald Trump's victory. They'd been working all day at polling centres, getting out as much of the vote as they could, and had stayed up bleary eyed watching the results come in. When it came to the inauguration they watched it live in the local doughnut shop and then that night they all went to one of the ladies' homes and watched a recording of the entire ceremony all over again. They had managed to procure a life-size cardboard cut-out of President Trump and they all posed for photos with it.

Jean is just 'delighted'.

'You know, I think he's doing an amazing job, in all honesty. The swiftness in which he gets things done is really impressive because it is Washington DC and they do tend to drag their feet a bit. Sometimes they do it intentionally and sometimes it's just a matter of having to go through all the procedure. But for what he's accomplished … I'm very impressed with what he's gotten done so far.' The only thing she's a little unsure of is the changes that the president and Republicans in Congress have been making to the Affordable Healthcare Act, how they're replacing the coverage provided under Obamacare.

While established politicos have been disturbed by the lack of experienced operatives and personnel in President Trump's inner circle, and by how his chief advisers appear to be his daughter Ivanka and her husband Jared – neither of whom have any government or foreign-policy experience – Jean has no such qualms.

'Every president brings their own crew with them. It's absolutely nothing different than any other administration. Look at the Kennedys. Everybody loved the Kennedys, right? Ted was working, Jack was president, Robert was the attorney general. I mean, this is nothing new. However, I think the press like to point things out that … They like to talk about nepotism and whatnot, but it's very common. I mean, you're the president of the United States, you need people around you that you can trust.'

For those still struggling to understand Trump, there is some insight to be gleaned from the first two paragraphs of the first page of his 1987 business biography, *The Art of the Deal*, which he wrote with Tony Schwartz (although Mr Schwartz alleges that Donald Trump actually wrote very little of it). It explains exactly his business modus operandi then as a New York real-estate wheeler and dealer and it seems to explain exactly his modus operandi as president in 2017.

'I don't do it for the money. I've got enough, much more than I'll ever need. I do it to do it. Deals are my art form. Other people paint beautifully on canvas or write wonderful poetry. I like making deals, preferably big deals. That's how I get my kicks.

'Most people are surprised by the way I work. I play it very loose. I don't carry a briefcase. I try not to schedule too many meetings. I leave my door open. You can't be imaginative or entrepreneurial if you've got too much structure. I prefer to come to work each day and just see what develops.'

That freewheeling element is visible in how he runs his White House.

———

What is missing from these pages is a discussion of foreign policy and whether voters made up their mind based on the foreign-policy positions of the candidates. That is not an accident: it is an accurate reflection of the voters I met and the issues they raised. Only on rare occasions did anything related to the outward-looking views of the US come up. And that was something else the Trump campaign tapped into – many Americans do not care for the theory of 'America as the world's policeman': they care more about the duty of the president to provide for the welfare of the American people first and foremost. This is particularly true of the Americans that Donald Trump targeted for votes. With Hillary Clinton's record as a Secretary of State, and the controversy surrounding the Benghazi attack, Donald Trump was able to frame her as an internationalist and himself as an American protectionist.

Then candidate Trump summed this up in his speech to the Republican National Convention when accepting his party's nomination in July 2016. 'Tonight, I will share with you my plan of action for America. The most important difference between our plan and that of our opponent is that our plan will put America first. Americanism, not globalism, will be our credo. As long as we are led by politicians who will not put America first, then we can be assured that other nations will not treat America with the respect that we deserve.'

This was a theme he solidified in his inaugural address on 20 January 2017: 'We assembled here today are issuing a new decree to be heard in every city, in every foreign capital and in every hall of power. From this day forward, a new vision will govern our land. From this moment on, it's going to be America First. Every decision on trade, on taxes, on immigration, on foreign affairs, will be made to benefit American workers and American families.'

Military families would say they want an end to US interventionism, but generally it is not for greater US exchequer reasons or for the cause of 'world peace': it is for reasons closer to home. Families and friends are tired of burying 'our boys and our girls', tired of caring for veterans and battling over benefits. But the truth is that the military is the one and only way for very many people in this country to be able to afford a college education.

Despite the undoubted appeal Trump had, as evidenced in the words of his voters and his comprehensive victory, it remains true that the majority of Americans did not vote for him. In Michigan, Trump won by only 10,704 votes. Clinton won California by 3.4

million votes. Those 10,000 people in Michigan did more for Trump than millions of Californians did for Clinton.

Meeting some of those voters, realising that they have justifiable reasons for being attracted to Trump, and remaining attracted to him despite actions that others consider intolerable or scandalous, is key to understanding the Trump phenomenon a little better. America is now at a crossroads, both politically on the domestic front and in terms of re-establishing its place in the world. Does it want to be inward looking? To put 'America First'? Will that create the jobs so many people crave? As Trump moves America to be more protectionist, more isolationist, will that phenomenon spread? Will we see 'Ireland First' posters at our next general election? Do facts matter anymore, or is it more about a feeling of truth rather than the truth? Donald Trump has changed the way campaigns and elections will be run for ever more. A man who in 140 characters can reach more people than all of the US television networks combined and not pay a dollar for it. A candidate who can get all the way to the White House and well into his presidency without articulating core policies in any substantive way apart from catch-calls and rally cries. He has both emasculated the media and spurred what may just be a golden age of journalism. And on 18 February 2017, four weeks and one day after he was sworn into office, he held a 'campaign rally' in Florida. And so it began. The unofficial launch – in his own mind on that particular day, anyway – of Trump 2020.

President Trump faces many challenges: while he had a stunning victory, one that will be parsed and analysed for years if not decades to come, he is not riding in on a wave of consensus. He enjoyed no honeymoon period. He faces challenges from all sides: challenges coming from the majority of the country that did not vote for him – not just the popular majority that Clinton enjoyed, but the fact that only 61.4 per cent of voting-age Americans voted in the first place; challenges coming from within his own party – the conservative 'Never Trump' movement; and, crucially, the biggest challenge of all may come from his inability to fulfil his own promises. He dreamed big, and people bought what he was selling: now he has to deliver. However, governing is not campaigning and in the early months his inexperience and that of those around him have resulted in some unforced errors and self-inflicted injuries.

The White House resembles a bullet-strewn battleship at times, such is the widespread nature of the 'leaks' coming from disgruntled career civil servants. His administration appears neither calm nor in control. He is admirably trying to stick to his promises of applying his business methods and deal-making regimes to the business of government, but the transition is not that simple. He is operating akin to the boss of a mom-and-pop business (albeit a big one), just as he has all his professional life. He's never had to answer to shareholders before, but now he has the American people. He's never had conflicting power sources before, but now he has Congress and the judiciary. While the political system in Washington DC can be criticised for lethargy and stagnation, the separation-of-powers design is providing checks on the power of the president just as the Founding Fathers intended, irrespective of the obvious frustration it is causing to those involved in the Trump administration.

While some of those disappointed with the outcome have maintained 'the resistance', a great many have swallowed their reservations and rowed in for the greater good, for the love of country, behind a democratically elected president.

That esprit de corps was clearly displayed by the boycotting Ohio Republican governor John Kasich. Despite not having voted for President Trump, Mr Kasich was one of the first to visit him at the White House after the inauguration and declare a truce for the good of the country. He shared with White House reporters afterwards the advice he had passed along to the forty-fifth president.

'The man is the president of the United States. It's sort of like being on an airplane: you want to root for the pilot if you are on the airplane with the pilot. You don't want that pilot to screw up.'

At times during the contest John Kasich had been the voice of reason, and standing on the driveway of the White House, coming from a meeting in an office he'd hoped might have been his, he swallowed his pride and put patriotism front and centre.

'I remember back when I first became governor,' he said. 'There were some things that I was doing to the point where my wife said to me, "You are the father of Ohio, act like it." It takes time for people to get stabilised. We all wish this president the best. That does not mean that there might be things that I see that I don't agree with. I will say that. I am not trying to pull him down or anyone else down. I am not red or blue. I am red, white and blue. I want to put America first, not my party or some arcane ideology. If I can help my country, I am going to do what I can. That comes in various ways and packages.'

'I am red, white and blue' – that patriotic spirit, that national pride, goes to the heart of what happened in the 2016 election. It's what causes people to fly the star-spangled banner from their homes and in their gardens. It's what causes around 60,000 young people to sign up for the US military each year to be dispatched to townlands on the other side of the world they possibly have never heard of and probably can't pronounce. It's what causes people to have patriotic symbols tattooed on their body. It's what motivates people to pull together for the common good. It's what inspires people to want to Make America Great (Again).

The people who voted for Donald Trump were statistically the poorer, less well off, less educated, rural, older, whiter populations. However, limiting the description of them to those demographic labels alone is to do a disservice to the voters and to President Trump. His voters were also largely the alienated. Those who felt the country had moved off without them. Those who felt career politicians had left them behind in place of self-aggrandisement. Those who felt the prospect of the American Dream had moved even further from their grasp. Just as the traditional political parties in Europe have experienced in a heightened way themselves in 2017, the underlying lesson from the 2016 US presidential election is: do not underestimate the electorate. Do not ignore vast swathes of the population. Misjudge voters at your peril.

NOTES

1   Carole Coleman, *The Battle for the White House … and the Soul of America* (The Liffey Press, 2008).

2   Statistics taken from the exit poll carried out by Edison Research for the National Election Pool.

3   https://www.census.gov/content/dam/Census/library/publications/2016/demo/acsbr15-01.pdf

4   Richard Florida, *The New Urban Crisis: How Our Cities Are Increasing Inequality, Deepening Segregation, and Failing the Middle Class – and What We Can Do about It* (Basic Books, 2017).

5   As of 2015, the most recent available figures from the US Census Bureau.

6   *Observer-Reporter*, style supplement, 9 November 1986. Accessed 25 March 2017 https://news.google.com/newspapers?nid=2519&dat=19861109&id=f7BdAAAAIBAJ&sjid=vloNAA AAIBAJ&pg=2115,1709800&hl=en

7   Statistics all taken from the Customs and Border Patrol Agency annual reports available at https://www.cbp.gov/newsroom/media-resources/stats#

8   Much debate has gone on in the media about the terms 'illegal' and 'undocumented' and each conveys something of a political agenda. Both are in fact correct. The presence of the immigrants is illegal – they have broken the law by entering the US by unlawful methods, without passing through border control and without a visa/permission. However, it is not breaking the law on the level of murder, rape or any other serious crime. Many have done so in search of a better of life for themselves. They are also undocumented, in that they do not have the correct documentation to be in the US and to be working there, but it is perhaps a kinder term and doesn't imply that all of those who come to the US outside of the regularised entry process are the 'bad guys' – or, as President Trump once said, 'bad hombres'. In my work as a journalist for a publicly funded broadcaster, and by extension in writing this book, I do not take sides on this debate. Thus I use both terms interchangeably.

9   According to the latest information from the Pew Research Foundation.

10   Letters to the Editor, Review Section, *New York Times*, Sunday April 1st 2016 https://www.nytimes.com/2017/04/01/opinion/sunday/abortion-and-the-democrats.html?_r=0

11   United States Conference of Catholic Bishops, 'Forming Consciences for Faithful Citizenship'. Accessed 21 June 2017. http://www.usccb.org/issues-and-action/faithful-citizenship/forming-consciences-for-faithful-citizenship-part-one.cfm

12   *Washington Post*, 16 March 2017. Accessed 21 June 2017. https://www.washingtonpost.com/news/to-your-health/wp/2017/03/16/drugs-are-killing-so-many-in-this-county-that-cold-storage-trailers-are-being-used-as-morgues/?utm_term=.a567af6f6101

13   Accessed   21   June   2017.   https://www.facebook.com/cityofeastliverpool/
      posts/879927698809767

14   Jay Richardson, 'Cherry Tree Myth', Digital Encyclopedia of George Washington.
      Accessed   21   April   2017.   http://www.mountvernon.org/digital-encyclopedia/
      article/cherry-tree-myth/#_edn1

15   Not to beat up on Bland County – the Appalachian Trail Conservancy describes
      it as follows: 'Bland County is a recreational paradise, and along with the rest of
      southwest Virginia, is becoming a hub for tourism. The scenic vistas, historical
      landmarks, outdoor activities, and abundant rivers, lakes and streams make this
      area a mecca for visitors.' Accessed 22 June 2017. http://www.appalachiantrail.org/
      home/conservation/a-t-community-program/at-community-partners/bland-
      county-va

16   Donald J. Trump with Tony Schwartz, *The Art of the Deal* (Ballantine Books,
      1987), p. 173.

17   You can follow the movements of Manhattan, Montauk and friends by using the
      Global Shark Tracker tool provided by Ocearch on its website, www.ocearch.org

18   Figures correct as of March 2017.

19   Figures correct as of April 2017.

20   According to the US National Community Survey, September 2016.

21   'Christians Who Are in North Carolina'. Accessed 23 June 2017. http://www.
      pewforum.org/religious-landscape-study/state/north-carolina/christians/
      christian/

22   Labor Force Statistics from the Current Population Survey: A-38. Persons not
      in the labor force by desire and availability for work, age, and sex. Most recent
      figures available for May 2017.   https://www.bls.gov/web/empsit/cpseea38.htm
      Accessed July 6 2017.

23   Multiple investigations are ongoing into Russian interference in the 2016 US
      presidential elections and possible collusion with the Trump campaign. While
      the US intelligence community is mostly united in its belief that there was
      interference, they do not believe that amounted to physical vote tampering, but
      rather was a cyber campaign designed to influence voters rather than alter ballot
      papers.

24   According to the states that Donald Trump won on election night, he should have
      accumulated 306 votes; however, when it came for the electoral-college votes to
      be officially cast, two members of the electoral college in Texas did not cast their
      votes for him, thus history will record him as having won 304 electoral-college
      votes.

25   As with Donald Trump, Hillary Clinton won 232 electoral-college votes based on
      the results of election night; however, when it came to formally cast the votes, five
      electors, four from Washington and one from Hawaii, withheld those votes that
      had been pledged to her, so history will record her official victory as 227.

26   David J Garrow, *Risng Star: The Making of Barack Obama* (William Morrow,
      2017).